THE DREAM OF DESCARTES

JACQUES MARITAIN

The Dream of

Descartes

together with some other
ESSAYS

Translated by MABELLE L. ANDISON

PHILOSOPHICAL LIBRARY

NEW YORK

ISBN 978-0-8065-3086-4

Printed in the U.S.A.

By F. Hubner & Co., Inc., New York, N. Y.

TABLE OF CONTENTS

PAGE

Preface 9

Chapter   I.—The Dream of Descartes............. 11

II.—The Revelation of Science........... 31

III.—The Deposition of Wisdom.......... 59

IV.—The Cartesian Proofs of God......... 105

V.—The Cartesian Heritage.............. 161

Notes 187

TO PIERRE VAN DER MEER
DE WALCHEREN

PREFACE

I should like to have devoted a whole comprehensive work to Descartes; but having little hope of finding the leisure necessary for that purpose, I have decided to gather together at this time, some studies bearing only upon certain aspects of the Cartesian system, but dealing with some important problems. The first three chapters appeared as articles in 1920 and 1922. The fifth is a lecture which seemed as though it might serve as conclusion. The fourth was written for this volume.

What I have attempted to do in this book is to try to determine the value and significance of the Cartesian reform with regard to metaphysical and theological wisdom; and that is what creates the unity between the diverse studies of which it is composed. Added to the chapter devoted to Descartes in THREE REFORMERS, *it specifies, I hope, in a sufficiently clear manner the data of a problem more up-to-date than ever, in my opinion.*

The figure of Descartes dominates all philosophy of the past three centuries, his historical significance is inexhaustible; the Cartesian attempt was magnificently carried out. But what M. Etienne Gilson wrote recently in regard to the cogito *can be applied in a general manner to that tragic experience, classical rationalism: "The Cartesian experiment was an admirable metaphysical undertaking bearing the hall-mark of genius; we owe it a great deal, if only for having brilliantly proven that any experiment of that nature is doomed ahead of time to failure . . ."**

---

* E. Gilson, *Le Réalisme Méthodique*, in Philosophia perennis, vol. II, p. 748.

The men of today have the very instructive privilege of watching the historic failure of three centuries of rationalism. It would be suicidal to blame reason. But they can observe everywhere, even in the economic order, what is produced by the claim of imposing upon matter the rule of a reason which itself refuses to be guided by the highest and most essential realities, and will be satisfied only with facile clarities. All rationalization *inevitably engenders absurd results when it is not the work of an integral reason, which heeds the order of wisdom and of nature.*

If one takes up one's position from the viewpoint of what might be called the sociology of the mind, and if one takes into account the cultural conditions at the beginning of the seventeenth century, in particular the human power of univocal prejudices which, immobilizing wisdom, bound it to an out-of-date idea of the science of the tangible world, the revolutionary work of Descartes appears as a great BLOCKADE-LIFTING *task, historically necessary. For good and for evil that work has produced its effects, it is not a question of trying to erase it from the pages of history. But it is certain that today reason can work usefully at the general reform everyone feels so necessary only if it first of all cures itself of Cartesian errors.*

CHAPTER I

THE DREAM OF DESCARTES

By JACQUES MARITAIN

Trans. by MABELLE L. ANDISON

CHAPTER I

THE DREAM OF DESCARTES

In the month of November, 1619, Descartes went into retirement in winter quarters near Ulm, following his attendance at the coronation of the Emperor Ferdinand at Frankfurt. Twenty-three years old at the time, the young soldier-philosopher was in the thick of his intellectual activity and scientific enthusiasm; in fact, his biographer does not hesitate to say that his brain was greatly over-stimulated.[1] He had spent the previous twenty months under the exciting influence of his friend, Isaac Beeckman[2]—"I was asleep and you wakened me," Descartes wrote him—and had dedicated his first work, *Compendium Musicae* (December, 1618) to him; and he turned back to his studies of physics and mathematics with keen interest. The beginning of his retirement was marked by an extraordinary occurrence: *X Novembris 1619*, he recorded in the daily account he kept in his youth[3]—*cum plenus forem Enthusiasmo, et mirabilis Scientiae fundamenta reperirem* . . . The tenth of November 1619, he was filled with Enthusiasm, he discovered the foundations of the Admirable Science, and at the same time his vocation was revealed to him in a dream.[4]

Descartes took great care to write out a minute description of this dream, in three parts; Baillet read it carefully and summarized it. To our profane eyes it may appear insignificant,

13

even absurd; the philosopher, however, looked upon it as completely supernatural.

Descartes dreams first of all that a tempestuous wind is whirling him about in the street as he struggles, hardly able to keep his feet, to reach the church of the College (of La Flèche) to say his prayers; at the very moment he turns to show courtesy to a man he had neglected to greet, the wind blows him violently against the Church; soon someone, in the middle of the college courtyard, tells him that an acquaintance of his has something— a melon—to give him . . . He experiences pain upon awakening, turns over on his right side, and prays God for protection against the bad effect of his dream. After that, falling asleep once more, he has another dream that fills him with terror; he is awakened by a burst of noise like a crack of lightning and sees thousands of sparks in his room. In a third and final dream he sees upon his table a Dictionary and a *Corpus poetarum,* open at a passage of Ausonius: *quod vitae sectabor iter?* (What path shall I follow in life?) An unknown man hands him a bit of verse—the words *Est et Non* catch his eye.

After several disconnected incidents too unimportant to relate, Descartes decides in his sleep that it is a dream, and interprets it. The interpretation obviously merits much greater attention than the dream itself; unfortunately, what comes to us through Baillet amounts to only a few very insufficient particulars.[5] We gather that the Dictionary signifies "all the various sciences grouped together," and that the *Corpus poetarum* "marks particularly and in a very distinct manner, Philosophy and Wisdom linked together." The words *Est et Non,* which are the "Yes and No of Pythagoras," represent "Truth and Falsity in human attainment and in secular sciences"; the section beginning

14

with *Quod vitae sectabor iter?* "marks the good advice of a wise person, or even moral theology." As to the wind that hurries the future author of the *Traité du monde* toward the College Church, it is an evil genius which, according to Baillet, "was trying to throw him by force into a place where it was his design to go voluntarily"—*a malo spiritu ad Templum propelle-bar,* wrote Descartes,[6] without telling us what Temple it was, symbolized by the Chapel in the College of La Flèche. The melon is the love of that solitude Descartes reproaches himself with having sought up till then, for purely human reasons. This melon highly amused the eighteenth century readers of the Life of the philosopher.

Finally, the lightning is "the Spirit of Truth that descended upon him and took possession of him."

Descartes, Baillet tells us, took the first two dreams as a warning about his past life—the last, as a revelation bearing upon the future. It was the Spirit of Truth, he knew beyond all doubt, that wanted "to open for him, by this dream, the treasure of all the sciences." And what is even more extraordinary, Des-cartes added that "the genius that heightened in him the enthusiasm which had been burning within him for the past several days, *had forecast these dreams to him before he had retired to his bed."* The historians of rationalism ought to settle for us once and for all, the identity of this Genius. Could it be by any chance, cousin to the *Mischievous Genius of the Meditations?*

The next day Descartes made the vow[7] fulfilled five years later,[8] to make a pilgrimage of thanksgiving to Lorette.

It is undeniably very annoying to find at the origin of modern philosophy a "cerebral episode," to quote Auguste Comte, which would call forth from our savants, should they meet it in the life of some devout personage, the most disquieting neuropathological diagnosis; and one can understand the dissatisfaction of these philosophical people in reading Baillet's account. "The Life of M. Descartes by M. Baillet," wrote Malebranche, "is bound to render him and his philosophy ridiculous." Huygens, strongly endorsed by Leibnitz, wrote in his turn: "The passage in which he relates how his brain was over-stimulated and in a fit state for visions, and his vow to Our Lady of Lorette, shows great weakness; and I think it will appear so, even to Catholics who have rid themselves of superstition." Even and above all to Catholics, kind and scholarly Huygens! Any dealing with Genii who instigate dreams can for them never be anything else than suspect.

As a matter of fact, the affair appears disconcerting. Baillet sympathetically strives to reduce the whole thing to a passing exhaustion due to mental strain. "He tired himself to such an extent that his brain became overheated and he fell into a kind of rapture which so worked upon his already exhausted spirit that it became predisposed to the reception of dreams and visions." Mr. Charles Adam now announces, in a tone as resigned as it is detached, that "an outburst or an attack of mysticism" is perhaps necessary to lift philosophers "out of themselves, above themselves," and to lead them to "a new vision of the truth."[9] At which Mr. Gaston Milhaud, who also speaks of a "mystic critis," and who quite rightly calls attention to the capital importance of that crisis in the origin of Cartesian philosophy, remarks with equal justice that a mental depression due to intellectual overexertion is not altogether the best way to raise intellectual strength to the point of obtaining "a new vision of truth," and to reveal at one stroke to the great reformer of philosophy the *foundations of the admirable science.*

*

*   *

As a matter of fact that state of intellectual quivering and "enthusiasm" in which Descartes found himself would be more easily explained if one were to admit with one of his recent biographers, Mr. Charles Adam, that if he had not just then become initiated (as Leibnitz was, later) into the brotherhood of the Rosicrucians, at least he had begun to move in their circle. In the long explanation Baillet gives his readers to clear Descartes of the accusation (brought against him on his return to Paris in 1623) of having joined the Rosicrucian brothers in Germany, does he not tell us that during his seclusion in the winter of 1619-1620, the philosopher, who "never refused his welcome to those amateurs able to discuss the sciences and the latest in literature," had "felt stirring within him an emulation" of the Rosicrucians (of whom he had heard such marvelous reports) "which moved him all the more deeply because accounts of them had reached him at the moment of his greatest perplexity concerning the means he should take in his search for truth"—that is to say, at the very moment of his *crisis?* Descartes therefore "set about finding one of those new savants in order that he might get to know them himself, and converse with them." Baillet, reverent apologist that he is, hastens to add that "all his trouble came to naught" and that "he was unable to find a single man who would admit being a member of the brotherhood, or who was even suspected of being one."[10] We know nevertheless, that during the entire winter of 1619-1620 Descartes was in close

17

scientific relationship with the mathematician Faulhaber, a professor at Ulm.[11] Now Faulhaber was a real Rosicrucian and a very ardent one,[12] and one is justified in assuming, in spite of Baillet's denials, that Descartes found in him the man he was seeking, and that through him Descartes entered into direct contact with the intellectual atmosphere of the Rosicrucians. Might not such contact, however fleeting, have had a deciding influence upon the moral lines and the aims of the philospher's life? May we not even ask ourselves whether at its origin Descartes' great idea did not permit the supposition that he intended—an intention which became hazier as time went on—fearlessly to transpose to the plane of everyday reason and of *the most widespread common sense* the design followed on the plane of alchemic mysteries by the naïve Rosicrucians, and in so doing to render it much less "uplifted," but much more efficacious—mathematics replacing the Cabala leading to universal Knowledge, the hermetic sciences and their occult qualities giving place henceforth to geometric Physics and the art of Mechanics, as the elixir of life to the laws of rational Medicine? Was it thus that, propelled by the mischievous genius toward the Temple of Knowledge where it was his intention to go voluntarily, or in other words, attracted momentarily by the Rosicrucian science, the philosopher rid himself of the evil temptation in order to reach the courts of Science by himself and by his reason alone?

Unfortunately all this is pure conjecture, and in spite of their likelihood the relations of Descartes with that mysterious brotherhood, which excited so much vain curiosity in the seventeenth century, remain in the category of historical hypotheses. The one thing that can be asserted definitely is that Descartes in 1619-1620 had a most lively curiosity to know the Rosicrucians, and that he was therefore "perfectly aware of the rumors circulated about them throughout the whole of Germany." All that he heard ascribed to that brotherhood whose aim was "the general reformation of the world, not in religion, in government or in morals, but only in the sciences," and his ardent preoccupation regarding it must have played a not unimportant part in the intellectual over-stimulation of those first few days in November 1619.

*

* *

Whatever may have been the relations between Descartes and the Rosicrucians, the thing that has the greatest interest for us is the discovery he made the tenth of November 1619, it is that "admirable science" whose foundations he found with the help of the "Genius" who "for several days past" . . . "had aroused Enthusiasm in him."

Is it simply a question of a mathematical invention, the discovery of analytical geometry, or that bold stroke by which he believed he might fuse the diverse mathematical sciences into one single science of proportions, or a question of the invention of the four rules of Method, or even the intuition of a sort of symbolism analogous to the *universal characteristic* of Leibnitz- Mr. Milhaud, in the very conscientious studies he devoted shortly before his death to the "crisis" of Descartes, and to which we have already alluded, treats these hypotheses as they deserve. There is nothing whatsoever in Descartes' juvenilia which has any bearing either upon the idea of a symbolism of concepts, the determination of the rules of Method, the idea of "general Algebra" or upon a universal mathematics. The great mathematical works and the discovery of analytical geometry are subsequent to the invention of the admirable science and consequently they must not be confused with it.[13] The "admirable science" represents something much more profound and universal.

In the *Discours de la Méthode* Descartes tells us in his clear, forceful style that it was precisely during his retirement in the winter of 1619 that he solemnly resolved to search henceforth for knowledge within himself[14] and that he conceived his philosophical reform. Let us read that page again with close attention.

"I would stay shut up by myself all day long in a heated chamber where I had ample leisure to commune with my own thoughts. One of the first of these was that I found myself considering that there is often not as much perfection in works composed of several parts and done by the hands of diverse masters, as in those in which one man alone has labored . . . And in like manner the thought came to me that since we have all been children before being men, and since for a long time we have had to be governed by our appetites and our preceptors which were often at variance with one another, and neither of which always gave us the best advice, it is almost impossible for our judgment to be as pure or as sound as it might have been if we had had unimpaired the full use of our reason from the time of our birth, and if we had been guided by it alone . . .

"As a result of these reflections, it was borne in upon me . . . that as far as all the opinions I had received thus far were concerned, I could not do better than to undertake once and for all to get rid of them, in order to replace them later with other and better ones, or even with the same opinions, once I had adjusted them to the level of reason."

THE DREAM OF DESCARTES

Let us compare the indications furnished by these passages with those Baillet gives us, according to the *Olympica*, concerning the dream of November tenth, 1619, and the interpretation of it with which Descartes was inspired. Of the two books presented to him, one signified "all the sciences *gathered together*," and the other more precisely, "Philosophy and Wisdom *joined together*." Let us remember that the *Discourse on Method* was originally to have borne the title: *Project of a Universal Science Destined to Raise our Nature to its Highest Degree of Perfection*,[15] and that the dream of 1619 by which Descartes received his philosophic mission, and in which the Spirit of Truth opened to him the treasure of all the sciences, wherein "the human mind played no part," disclosed precisely to the philosopher "the foundations of the *admirable Science*," *mirabilis scientiae fundamenta*. Let us remember above all that the meditations which followed the dream (November 1619 to March 1620) are at the very source of all Cartesian philosophy, and that Descartes held the dream itself to be an event so decisive that he believed it "the most important thing in his life," and that he looked forward to offering reverent thanksgiving by a pilgrimage he was to make on foot from Venice to Lorette.

However cloaked in reticence the information contained in the *Discourse* may be, however dry and meaningless the "dreams" of 1619 may have become in Baillet's prosaic account, it is not impossible to discern behind these inanimate texts the intellectual drama to which they refer, the lively and effective intuition, the simple and fertile idea, all sparkling with angelic lustre, that must have flashed upon the philosopher that night in November, that *beata nox* when in a little heated room in Germany the reform of reason was conceived.

Descartes bethinks himself of an idea, very simple and marvelously clear. He understands, he sees that Science should be the work of one person alone, *a work done by the hand of a single master*: "As it is certain beyond any doubt that the state of true religion, where *God alone* made all the ordinances, must be incomparably better-ordered than all the others."[16]

He sees also, and in the same flash, that humanity, which the efforts of all the ancients have been unable to "advance by a single step in the pursuit of wisdom,"[17]—humanity has been but a child up to the present, governed by its appetites and its preceptors, and consequently has been kept in a servile state, although it is the heir to whom the world is promised.

Man has therefore had many opinions so far; he has never had "the certain knowledge of anything";[17] there is nothing, absolutely nothing he has *known,* properly speaking. But now he reaches manhood, he becomes master of himself and capable of *adjusting* everything *to the level of reason.* And having reached the days of his plenitude he puts away childish things; he will speak, think and know like a man.

"The true principles by which we can attain the highest degree of wisdom, which constitutes the sovereign good of human life, are those I have put in this book,"[18] Descartes later wrote in the dedicatory epistle to the French edition of the *Principia philosophiae.* He also expressed the wish that the right-thinkers might finally understand *to what degree of wisdom, to what perfection of life and to what happiness* the truths propounded by him could lead. The knowledge possessed by a humanity which has reached its maturity will procure its happiness chiefly by Mechanics, Medicine and Ethics; it will be "practical" in fact, and will make us "masters and possessors of nature."[19]

THE DREAM OF DESCARTES

Descartes' mission is therefore quite clear. If the Spirit of Truth descends upon him like a thunderbolt, it is in order that he may consecrate himself to that Science. For it, if necessary, he will forego all human intercourse and the pleasures of life: *and I have put it above kingdoms and thrones, and held riches as naught compared to it—et praeposui illam regnis et sedibus, et devitias nihil esse duxi in comparatione illius.*[20]

For him indeed is reserved the definitive founding of Science, and his descendanas through the centuries[21] will have only to develop its truths. For it is in him, in very truth, that humanity becomes adult, and he it is who is to be the one and only "Engineer" of the modern city of the intellect, a city entirely geometrical and straight as a die, in no way resembling "those ancient cities which, having been at their inception mere straggling villages, have grown with the progress of time into great cities," and which "are generally so badly proportioned."

"Quod vitae sectabor iter?—What way shall I take through life?" That is the great and singular mission he undoubtedly would not have dared to undertake of his own accord, but for which his election was revealed to him by the Spirit of Truth.

He must therefore overturn and scatter to the four winds all that men had tried to build up through past ages, and must make a clean sweep of all thinking that has been possible up to his time: a heroic enterprise that he has no right to hold back from, but which it will never again be necessary to undertake; an enterprise that is, for the common run of mankind, more to be marvelled at than imitated, for "the resolution to rid one's self of all opinions previously received is not an example to be followed by everyone."[22] It is human knowledge he must reconstruct.

In the meantime he is alone—no one can help him; no master, no book, no century-old experience, no voice from the past that will speak to him. To what then will he have recourse? To his reason alone: not to the syllogizing reason of Doctors and Savants, but entirely to the instinctive reason received by man directly from nature, to the common sense that has no need of any special qualifications acquired through prolonged effort, increasing his intrinsic worth,[23] and that needs only good rules of method in order to reach the summit of knowledge and of wisdom. That is the significance of the *Corpus poetarum* presented to the philosopher as the symbol of highest knowledge.

Descartes saw then, in the enthusiasm and inspiration of the poets, a means of discovery incomparably more powerful than reason heavily armed and the logic of the philosophers.[24] We know, moreover, that Cartesian reason with its immediate knowledge of "simple natures," its innate ideas, its atoms of evidence, its claim to replace syllogism with a succession of discontinuous intuitions, and its quasi-Platonic attempt to reduce demonstration to the transcendental unity of a non-discursive intellection—briefly, with its angelic ambitions, had to remain something entirely different from the classical reason recognized in the human being by Aristotle and the Schoolmen.

Since reason taken in the state of nature is the sufficient instrument of all knowledge, reason on the other hand being perfectly one in each man, why should Science not be one, why should it not be of the very unity of the human mind? "All the sciences" ought therefore to be "drawn together," natural "Philosophy" and "Wisdom" or Metaphysics ought to be "joined together," as the symbols of the Dictionary and the *Corpus poetarum* teach. It is in the unity of the *admirable science,* which

24

will imply one single light and single mode of certitude, that "the Spirit of Truth" opens to the philosopher "the treasure of all the sciences." He must put aside the traditional idea of the specific diversity of the sciences,[25] a singularly grave decision whose effects are not yet fully realized. What Descartes is entrusted to give to men is a "universal science" embracing all things knowable in his perfect specific unity—THE SCIENCE.

This Science then, which men have been seeking in vain for so long, and which is now offered to him like a new land, on which he has only to set foot, this Science or Philosophy will be created effortlessly in the mind as soon as the mind, instead of spreading itself outwardly, shall be willing to *study within itself* in order there to become aware of the truth, the seeds of which are all there, inborn. Let it but be alert to choose within itself the ideas which cannot deceive (such for example, as those of geometric essences or of number) that is to say, ideas *easiest* to grasp, the *simplest,* and which can be *most distinctly repre-sented;* and let it but be alert to follow by perfect deduction the train of these ideas as they follow one after the other;[26] linking self-evident elements by means of evident perceptions, it cannot fail to succeed; it will arrive by an infallible route and an easy one, at the *Universal Knowledge which will raise our nature to its highest point of perfection,* which will make *even those who have never studied* capable *of understanding the most curious* and the most difficult *matters,* leading them to the fullness of "wisdom" and of "felicity," to the "sovereign good of human life."

*

*   *

THE DREAM OF DESCARTES

It is thus in our opinion, that Descartes perceived, caught up in a single intuition, the vital idea, the *logos spermatikos* of his philosophical reform.

The intuition of the admirable science contains in embryo the whole of Cartesian rationalism, and still more. It implies in the youth of twenty-three who is to lay anew the foundation of knowledge, an unusual strength of intellectual concentration, passion for truth, and energy of will, and a fearless self-confidence accompanied by a hyperbolical scorn for the past. It brings with it the out-and-out dogmatism which is to characterize—and compromise—the metaphysics of the moderns, and by way of reaction, lead to the arrogant injunctions of Kant, and the facile skepticism of "positive" minds. It presupposes the possibility of a single science accounting for everything, easily possessed by man, and bearing, as does mathematics, on intelligibles made to the measure of the mind. Above all it actually isolates the human mind in the creation of Science, which the mind deduces altogether from the seeds of truth innate in itself, and which, being true as well as being only an unfolding of our thought, becomes in fact the rule of reality. Thus, along with universal mathematism, it already instils the Cartesian doctrine of ideas and the Cartesian doctrine of evidence, the principles of modern idealism.

But the most remarkable feature of this discovery of the admirable science is that it comes from above, being given to Descartes in a dream in which "the human mind played no part." Lest any one think the philosopher was that day *plenus musto*, and "that he might have been drinking that evening before retiring to his bed" (as Huet was later basely to claim), he takes care to note down himself that he had had no wine to drink for three

26

months.[27] The enthusiasm which animates him in his solitude
has a divine origin, the intoxication of that night of November
tenth, 1619, is a holy intoxication, it is within him like a Pentecost
of Reason.

As this *scientia mirabilis* was a personal revelation to the
philosopher, we can more easily understand why the Cartesian
doctrine has retained in several important points the marks of
a kind of collusion between what is human knowledge and what
is revelation. In particular we can understand why Descartes
so often seems to conceive Philosophy on the pattern of Theology.
Many aspects of Cartesianism become clear in this light. The
manifold "simple natures" that are the principles from which
all knowledge is drawn, and that force themselves upon us
purely and simply, without allowing us to resolve them into a
more primordial and universal concept (such as the concept of
being for the ancients), are thus like the articles of faith of a
natural revelation whose instrument is reason,[28] "reason" itself
having in Descartes a rôle scarcely less divine than "conscience"
was later to have in Jean-Jacques Rousseau. The ontological
argument, which causes us immediately to grasp the existence of
God through the very idea we have of Him, is a substitute or
succedaneum of a revelation or a vision of God Himself. (Malebranche will undertake to show this.) The order followed by
Descartes in Physics, where he claims to deduce the first laws
of movement from the attributes of God, is nothing more or
less than the theological order—which proceeds from God to
the creature—improperly transposed to science.

Finally and above all, the notion Descartes had of science
itself indicates the strangest confusion of ideas. It is a science
purely human, since it is obtained through reason alone; but

instead of being an ensemble of different kinds of science, each having its own special degree of abstraction and intelligibility, its own principles and methods, and its own mode of certitude, it is a single universal science, completely one,[29] as is the science of God, Who sees everything in its essence. [30] Instead of resulting in the slow labor of generations, in the imperfect way of human things, which means both continued effort on the part of everyone and the magisterial authority, however precarious, of a few, it is established perfect at one stroke, by one man, just as the revelation was accomplished in its perfection by One alone, by the only Son, and as "the state of true religion" was "ordained by God alone." Instead of having as its supreme criterion the evidence of the object, and of resolving itself into real things by means of sense intuition, the source of all our knowledge, it resolves into divine truthfulness itself, like angelic knowledge, and it rests formally and above all on the authority of God the Author of clear ideas and Creator of our faculties of knowledge, just as supernatural faith has for its formal reason the authority of God the Author of revelation. Instead of being purely speculative, in so far as it studies nature, it is both speculative and practical like theology—*scientia eminenter speculatica et practica,* or rather it is first of all practical, and it will provide by itself "the sovereign good of human life," in giving us mastery of ourselves and of the world. Science as Descartes conceives it is a human science which would be at the same time divine by revelation, or better still, would be the very science of God and of the Angels. If this be so, it is no doubt by virtue of the idealism and, if I may use the word, of *the angelism* which in general characterizes Cartesian philosophy; but it is also that Knowledge always remained for Descartes the *science admirable*

28

of the tenth of November, 1619, and that his dream was for him truly the revelation of Knowledge.

Among the ideological elements the first seed of which was introduced by the Cartesian reform, and whose development,

*Having the expanding power of things infinite,**

changed during three centuries the intellectual universe of humanity, one of the most important is assuredly the idea of what the modern world calls The Science, with all the emotional and reverential complements evoked by this word.

This Science that plays in the mythology of modern times a rôle as majestic and as formidable as Progress itself, this Science that promised everything and denied everything, that raised above all things the absolute independence, the divine *aseity* of the human mind, and which has made so many men, led astray by it from the eternal verities, into sorrowful beings

C'hanno perduto il ben dello intelletto,

is not the true science, science such as it exists and is brought about by scientists, science submissive to things and to extramental reality. It is the Mid-Autumnal Night's Dream conjured up by a mischievous genius in a philosopher's brain—it is *the Dream of Descartes.*

* Baudelaire.

29

CHAPTER II

THE REVELATION OF SCIENCE

CHAPTER II

THE REVELATION OF SCIENCE

What is the true countenance of Descartes? What is the real meaning of his *reform?* This problem will ever be with us and will always concern us. But its aspect varies with the times. Victor Cousin, if he did not exaggerate the historical importance of the philosopher, at least misunderstood it and presented it in much too one-sided and too arbitrary a manner; he saw in Descartes the liberator of philosophy which up to that time had been enslaved. The rationalist school has taken delight in picturing him as the breaker of fetters suddenly come down from heaven to sunder the chains of dogma and to set reason free; one who confronting as a demi-god an age still under the yoke of authority derives all his strength from himself alone.

Recent scholarship has been successful in completely renovating these somewhat ingenuous points of view. Ever since the publication of the studies of Espinas, and especially since the appearance of the theses of Mr. Gilson and Mr. Blanchet, we have known that Cartesian thought developed in the midst of apologetic preoccupations, in an atmosphere charged with theology; we have known that it worked on traditional material and that it had nothing of an "absolute beginning"; and certainly numerous and curious discoveries are still assured to those who will pursue a detailed research of the relation of the ideas of Descartes

33

with the scholasticism of his time. Documents in hand, we see what might very well have been asserted *a priori:* namely, that even in the intellectual world there is no such thing as spontaneous generation. Indeed, in applying the axiom of Aristotelian physics to the succession of great philosophical systems, it would be much truer to say that the decay of one produces the birth of the other. Thus is revealed, in spite of Descartes, between him and his predecessors, a continuity whose scope will appear the more extended as the history of ideas becomes better known.[31]

That continuity is, however, a *material* continuity. It should not conceal the very real—and much more important—*formal* discontinuity marked by the advent of Cartesianism; nor should we, by one of those excesses so habitual to historical theories in their comings and goings, forget now that the Cartesian no less than the Lutheran reform was, substantially, a revolution. Likewise, in changes of substance, if there is continuity on the side of matter so that the "ultimate disposition" of the matter is common to the body that is ceasing to be and the one which is beginning to be, there is none-the-less discontinuity on the side of form, and that is the essential point: new substantial form, new substance, new being, new virtues, a production really new in the world.

From this point of view it might well be that the classical interpretation of the rationalist historians—"and at last Descartes appeared"—no matter how false in a literal sense, remains true on another level and in quite a different way than they think. Descartes brings something new—well does he know it—he knows it so well that, jealous to the extreme of his originality, he nevertheless uses a thousand ruses to cover up or to attenuate the novelty of the positions he boasts of having discovered.

LARVATUS PRODEO

Being by itself acts. *Privations* do not act, prosper and proliferate unless in virtue of the good they affect by accident.

In any doctrine, then, endowed with intellectual efficacy, and which has exerted a determinative influence on the history of thought, we must look for the virtue of being, the hidden presence, the expansive power of a certain truth. A presence which only too obviously does not suffice to signify innocence, since it is a characteristic of our human weakness to be able to contaminate and corrupt even the most lofty truths; evil, in virtue of the principle that it acts only through good, is never so efficacious as when it damages the summits of being.

From beneath the stern and mighty brow of Descartes shine two living truths, two precious truths—one that is old, the other new.

The latter is the young truth of physico-mathematical science, the former is that ancient truth, the Socratic and Christian precept: Go back into thyself and into the spiritual element which is within thee. Descartes, whose ability as a scientist can scarcely be exaggerated, not only felt or divined, and in fact utilized the resources of mathematics applied to the knowledge of nature—as for example did Galileo, and before him da Vinci—he also had the clear intellectual view of the inner structure and rights of physico-mathematical knowledge of the world, with all its exigencies and, if I may say so, its fierceness as an original discipline, an irreducible *habitus*. From that point of view he really deserves to be regarded as the founder of modern science—not that he created it out of nothing, but because it was he who brought it out into the bright light of day and set it up on its own in the republic of the mind.

On the other hand, at a time when decadent Aristotelianism, unable to maintain itself in the realm of the intellect, was becoming daily more and more the slave of outer appearances—I mean, was becoming obscured in an acrid cloud of opinions on phenomena and of confusedly empirical concepts—and was showing in practice, in its manner of procedure, that icy materialism which is the punishment of those called to wisdom when they play false, Descartes perceived with a simple glance (even too simple), the necessity of turning away from external appearances with their endless contradictions, in order to rise to the spiritual realities that self-knowledge reveals; a regression *ad intus,* a conversion of the spirit upon itself which, taken separately and considered in itself, was only a recalling of the great tradition of Plato and of St. Augustine, but the urgency[32] of which was revealed to the meditative mathematician in a gleam of discovery.

The success of Cartesianism is explained not only by its false clarities, but also and especially by the active presence in it of the two truths I have just mentioned. Perceived more or less confusedly, these truths fascinated and deceived the seventeenth century; and what more seductive than the dual prestige of science and spirituality? The philosophy of Descartes, "attractive and bold" as La Fontaine called it, came into the world with an appearance of Christian and geometric heroism, measuring the earth and immediately finding God in the soul. One can understand how Mr. de Bérulle in his search for a philosophy more modern than Scholasticism, based less upon reasoning and which would seem more adapted to the science of the times as well as to the inner needs of men's souls, when he heard Descartes at the Papal Nuncio's in 1628, thought he had discovered in him the man marked out for that great work of restoration. One can also understand how the former pupil of La Flèche nourished for so long the hope that he might win over his former masters, or failing this and turning for a moment toward the Sorbonne and toward the devout Platonists of the Oratory, he constructed his great work of metaphysics on the model of pious *meditations* and presented his philosophy under such a purely edifying and apologetic guise. And finally we can understand that today to certain enlightened souls whose perspicacity however does not seem to have been greatly sharpened by the lessons of almost three centuries of history, the work of Descartes continues to appear to be but the glorious advent of science and a praise-worthy spiritualist renewal.

Descartes must have harbored illusions on this point. Although the only thing he really cherished was his physics—it was for his physics above all, that he wrote the *Méditations,* in order to assure the success of mechanism by binding its fate to that of the knowledge of the soul and of God[33]—he believed quite sincerely that by his philosophy he was serving the interests of religion; still more, he was convinced he had given to the world a philosophy more Christian, more satisfying to the senti-ments of a Christian reader, more adapted to his standards, more palatable and more easy-of-access, in short more lovable for him than weighty Scholasticism burdened with the farrago of the tangible world.

Nevertheless a philosophy must be nothing but true; then and then only is it really Christian. It must not be lovable or made to the measure of some sentiment, even of the highest and purest sentiment, even of "Christian sentiment." It must conform to the measure of *what is;* and here we come up against the exigencies of the object. It is an excellent lesson in intellectual discipline to realize that a certain contamination of the reason by sentiment, even by religious sentiment itself and by the most laudable zeal, causing a certain lapse in the pure objectivity of the intelligence, has perhaps a share of the responsibility for the initial deviations of Descartes' thought, and for the very earliest formation of what was to become rationalism.

Descartes turns his vision inward; he shuts himself up within himself, *clauso ostio, in abscondito,* not to pray but to think, not to make his devotions but to philosophize; thus he transposes in the most curious way a procedure of Christian spirituality to the level of nature and of reason. And certainly silence is as necessary for philosophizing as it is for praying. But he who concentrates in prayer knows already by faith that God is present in his soul, and he seeks to rise above reason by an obscure but loving knowledge which will deliver him to the wholly spiritual action of this hidden God—or at least he seeks by meditation, to become imbued with truths already present within himself; that is why, withdrawing into himself, he closes all the doors of his heart.[34] The philosopher, on the contrary, undertakes to know things rationally, and if he withdraws into himself in meditation, it is in order to purify the scrutiny of his mind upon what exists, and not in order to forget the world of the senses, but to find within the human realm, already bordering on metaphysical realities, objects more intelligible and less bound up in matter; that is why, withdrawing into himself, he opens all the windows of his mind.

Now Descartes is philosophizing, and is not withdrawing in mental prayer; and in order to philosophize, he proceeds exactly as he would if he were withdrawing in mental prayer. Watch him as "now he closes his eyes," "stops up his ears," "shuts off all his senses," "even effaces all images of corporal things from his thought" . . . He closes all outlets and strives within himself and using only his reason to attain the real, in the same manner in which the man of prayer attains God within himself through love and the infused gifts of grace. Instead of following the natural movement of knowledge and beginning with the senses, which alone are in immediate touch with existence, in order to rise to the intellect, and instead of arriving at the intellect as it is in its real nature—that is to say, a faculty essentially relative to the non-Ego, essentially fixed upon the object, essentially apprehensive of being, and in which the immensity of the real penetrates immaterially, and whose act has as its immediate goal not its ideas but the natures of things rendered present within it—Descartes, making use of the artificial and violent procedure of voluntary doubt, introductory to the revelation of the *Cogito*, has the pretension, in a flight of pure intellect, of rising to the plane of the intellect without passing through the gate of the senses, the way fixed for us by nature. And that is how, mistaking the very essence of knowledge, he seizes intellection as if it were a thing or an object, not as the active and living assimilation of objects and things; he is then in Thought as though in a sealed-off, impenetrable world, shut in and fixed upon itself—a world whose correspondence to the real world is guaranteed only by the veracity of God. This turning toward the inner self and the mind no longer consists only in purifying the gaze of the intelligence, in bringing it to bear upon more purely intelligible objects. It fixes this gaze upon the intellect itself as upon the only object which can be immediately present to it, and it denies to that perception we have of the world through our senses any validity in knowledge. The philosophical truth that Descartes had perceived, turning into idealism[35] becomes the vehicle of an error.

As to physico-mathematical science, taken in itself, it was compatible with the system of the traditional disciplines in which it could very logically have made its place. However, it was in fact already orientated toward mechanism and turned against the waning Aristotelian philosophy; and that for all sorts of reasons that we have tried elsewhere to make clear,[36] the main one of which is, of course, both the special nature of the new science—a mathematical translation of sense phenomena—and the very propensity of our intelligence toward being, which throws the physico-mathematician into what one might call a natural illusion, and makes him mistake the quantitative aspects he is considering and the mathematical entities he is manipulating for actually physical causes and principles. A quite privileged victim of that illusion which, with uncompromising obstinacy, he pushes to its final consequences, convinced that physics "is only geomerty," and making of physico-mathematical science natural philosophy itself, Descartes consummates the rupture between the new science and the former wisdom, and he rivets it for several centuries to the most hypocritically tryrannical and most deceiving of metaphysical postulates—to the postulates of a universal mathematism. The scientific truth he brought forth into the light of day, changing into mechanicism, becomes in its turn the vehicle of an error.

The two truths whose presence vivifies the Cartesian reform therefore serve another master, they are the mask of a hidden principle. Cartesian philosophy is a philosophy behind a mask.

In the juvenilia of Descartes we find the phrase *Larvatus prodeo.* "Like an actor wearing a mask, I come forward, masked, on the stage of the world."[37]

We shall not interpret this strange avowal either in the manifestly too gentle sense that Mr. Milhaud[38] attributes to it when he sees in it the simple allusion to the fact that although seemingly absorbed by his occupations of traveller and soldier, Descartes is in reality thinking of science; or in the sense at once too hard and too romantic that one might give it in assuming some deep mysterious plan bound up with that affiliation with the Rosicrucians which seems so probable to Mr. Gustave Cohen and to Mr. Charles Adam. For us, it is nothing more than the sign of one of the most profound and most typical characteristics of Descartes' own philosophy.

Let us grant Mr. Milhaud all he asks us to believe about Descartes' sincerity: Descartes was not a hypocrite, he did not try to mislead people—and that, after all, is merely refuting a rather crude hypothesis. But that does not prevent us from noting the ambiguity of his system, or even from admiring the diplomatic skill with which the philosopher conducted his operations.

We know what precautions he took and what strategy he

41

employed in order to present his system to the public of his time, and to assure its success. Was this merely a wise precaution in the face of the aggressive prejudices of the crowd and of the official savants? Most assuredly—but seeing him push that prudence to such lengths, seek expedients in order not to "stun people's imaginations" or to "shock generally accepted opinions,"[39] and seeing him retain only half of the double precept addressed to the children of light, calls to mind Bossuet's remark: "M. Descartes has always been afraid of being reprimanded by the Church, and to avoid that, he is known to take excessive precautions."[40] As Mr. Blondel puts it:[41] ". . . he pushes his doctrine imperceptibly by 'tacking' as much as is necessary so as always to have at his disposal the means of disavowing what he has put forward,[42] provided that he gets what he wants without endangering his position,"[43] never venturing "anything against the will of those in power."[44]

"Was it necessary," he wrote to his disciple Regius,[45] "for you to go ahead and reject so publicly the substantial forms and real qualities? Did you not remember that I had declared in express terms in my *Traité des Météores* that I did not discard them and that I did not claim to deny them, but only that they were not necessary to explain my thought, and that I could make my reasons understood without them?"—To affirm heliocentrism without incurring the same difficulties as Galileo, he claims to teach that the earth is motionless[46]—although it revolves about the sun—for the reason that the atmosphere of the earth is carried along with it, and that movement signifies only a displacement with regard to the immediately neighboring body. And I am perfectly aware that this manner of speaking is in accord with his theory of movement, but still he was not ignorant

42

of the fact that in every-day language a cork carried along by the current is not motionless, and the artifice he uses here is a little lacking in elegance. When he is afraid that the Society of Jesus might turn against him, he threatens to draw up a parallel of the philosophy of the Schoolmen and his own philosophy, where, as Baillet says, those who had not learned the philosophy of the School would learn it much more easily than from their masters, and by the same means, would learn to despise it.[47] When it is a question however, of winning over the Jesuit Fathers to whom he makes it known that "his own inclination and the consideration of his duty lead him passionately to desire their friendship,"[48] he does not hesitate to declare that his principles can be utilized in Christian teaching "without going contrary to the text of Aristotle."[49] Nor does he hesitate to write to Father Charlet:[50] "I know people have thought my opinions were new, and yet it will be seen here that I make use of no principle which has not been accepted by Aristotle and by all those who ever undertook to philosophize"—of course, it is to be understood that he is using only the principles of "common sense," and that he is casting aside all the specifically philosophic principles of Aristotle and the rest. And so by a lucky chance he finds it possible in the *Principia Philosophiae* (which he writes so that the Fathers can use them in their colleges) to declare himself partisan of that *indifference* which in the *Méditations* he had declared foreign to the freedom of human will, and to which he knows the Society to be so attached.

But all this concerns in short only devices of policy: subtleties, perhaps—not lies; mental reservations at most. And who would dare to condemn for so doing that shrewd and headstrong mind? Let us rather bear in mind that Descartes knew very well both the value of what he was bringing out and the formidable power of the irrational in man, especially in the Doctors who misuse theology to immobilize science. Bossuet could speak at his ease of the philosopher's anxieties; the Galileo affair was still warm. And yet, what Descartes also knew, or surmised only too well—and in this the remark made by Bossuet takes on all its force—was the profound incompatibility of his philosophy with the whole authentic tradition of Christian wisdom. And I say—and this is much more serious—that it is a characteristic of Cartesian thought itself to be a masked thought. Is it deliberately calculated to be so? Obviously not. But thought that is involuntarily ambiguous, therefore ambiguous in its essential mode of thought, is but the more insidious. Descartes' thought is cloaked in a double prestige, as we have seen, that of science and of apologetics, of geometry and of spirituality. His thought quite sincerely takes the part of religion against theists and libertines, and presents itself as Christian, and as such will be received; and yet its fundamental principles will develop into a sheer enmity of reason against faith. By intention, Descartes' philosophy is realistic, and by its theory of knowledge as by its *angelism,* it introduces into modern philosophy the germ of the most intense idealism. It is turned toward physical reality, which it wishes to submit to knowledge more perfectly than anyone has ever before dreamed of doing—and in isolating metaphysics from experience as in making the physical world the domain of mechanicism, it prepares the fatal separation in modern times of metaphysics from science. In the practical realm it is rooted in submission to the established order—and in the realm of intellectual speculation it brings about the triumph, willy-nilly, of the very principle of individualism.

May we be allowed at this point to dwell upon a curious way in which Cartesian philosophy proceeds: as Mr. Gilson [51] has remarked, it breaks the superior concilations in which the great antinomies of the real were resolved by Scholasticism into two contrasting pieces which it affirms separately and which it cannot reunite; and from there on at almost every point this philosophy places side by side a thesis and an antithesis equally extreme, one of which serves to mask the other. It declares, for example, that the idea of God is the clearest and most distinct of all our ideas, and claims to grasp the existence of God in His idea alone—and thus it inclines toward ontologism; but it also states that the infinite absolutely cannot be an object of knowledge, and that it is presumptuous to seek in things the mark of their ordination by the intelligence of God—and thus it inclines toward agnosticism.

This philosophy states in metaphysics that an atheist does not really know mathematics; and through the difficulties to which it gives rise concerning the notion of created causality, it prepares the way for the doctrine of God as sole agent, wherein Father Boursier[52] will unite Cartesianism and Jansenism; but in its aversion for the notion of finality, it puts the whole order of nature out of reach of the divine wisdom, and it reduces in physics, the controlling action of God to the "fillip" which Pascal speaks of.[53] If it refuses to recognize in God an Intellect *virtually distinct* from the will, and ordering the will—an Intellect in virtue of which He acts (so that in this philosophy God runs the risk of appearing to be a pure, efficient Omnipotence from Whom things spring forth into being at the demand of His nature—if it claims to *deduce* the first laws of physics from the

divine nature itself, to make up for it it then immediately
conceals this opening toward pantheism by affirming divine transcendence and freedom in so extreme a manner that it looks upon
the eternal essences themselves as being created, and holds that
God could have brought it about that circles were square. And
if in denying the distinction between potentiality and act in
things, and in giving of substance a definition that can be applied
only to divine substance it tends to make two absolutes of
Extension and Thought, and in so doing prepares the way for
Spinoza, nevertheless, in order immediately to maintain the
complete subordination of things with regard to God, it affirms
without delay the theory of continued creation which it borrows
from the Scholastics, but borrows only to distort.[54]

Cartesian philosophy maintains at one and the same time the
freedom of the will (to the point of attributing to it all
speculative errors) and the principle that the will always follows
the understanding (to the point of seeking in the understanding
the means sufficient for moral perfecting—"il suffit de bien juger
pour bien faire," correct action depends only on correct judgment)
but it "suppresses without replacing"[55] the solution by which
Scholastic philosophy conciliated these two theses.

It so definitely makes of the understanding and of the will
two forces really distinct in us that it explains the difference
between moral freedom and error by the difference in extent of
these two faculties, and attributes judgment to will, not to understanding. But it reduces feelings and affections to obscure ideas,
and, by denying the real distinction between substance and
accident, it effaces the faculties themselves and has the soul
consist entirely in Thought.

It states so definitely the distinction between soul and body, and the independence of the soul, that it renders their union and all action of the one upon the other quite incomprehensible; and it identifies the human person and the soul. But it explains all vegetative and sensitive life by the body alone, and will enable the materialism of La Mettrie to claim kinship with the Cartesian beast-machines.

One could go on lengthening the list of these oppositions that Descartes leaves for what they are in the rough, without making any effort to conciliate them. All these contrasting pieces, forever incapable of being united, are fragments of Christian wisdom, a Christian wisdom which not so long before had been living, although at a reduced pace, and now lay broken into several bits each one of which was to follow its own destiny. Let us not try to find out if in effect, and by reason of an irresistible historical law, the negative antitheses should not little by little prevail over the positive theses. Let us rather ask if these fragments do not bear witness to a cleaving action exerted by some powerful foreign body, by some adverse principle, by some incompossible Newness introduced by the reformer into the unity of Christian philosophy.

Is it possible to reveal and to define this newness which is spirit, movement, impulse, tendency? In any case we can grasp its first manifestation. It is the great intuition of November 1619, which contains within itself virtually all the rest, and which reveals to the philosopher in a supernatural flash the object to which he is to devote his life: Science—the admirable science in which unite and culminate both the splendor of physico-mathematical cognition—for it is a universal triumph of

mathematical clarity—and the splendor of spiritual interiority—
for it is an outflowing of the science of God in our spirit, a
sort of angelic geometry.

THE MYTH OF SCIENCE

Science according to Descartes is one, of the very unity of
thought. Thus he not only transposes into the order of intellectual
virtues what the ancients used to say of the *connection* of the
moral virtues,[56] but also he transforms that connection into
unity pure and simple, into the unity of one and the same specific
nature. "All the sciences brought together are nothing but human
wisdom, which is always one, always the same, no matter how
varied the subjects to which it may be applied." One can
doubtless distinguish different parts in Science, but as members
of one identical spiritual organism. And contrary to the most
obvious experience, where we see minds which cultivate
different intellectual virtues, seized by the specificity of the object
as by a cupping-glass, accentuate more and more their divergences
and become even more and more strangers to one another, it must
be stated that the different sciences are "so bound together that
it is easier to learn all of them than to learn one alone, separating
it from the others."[57] Here we see abolished that distinction—
the *specifically hierarchized* distinction between Metaphysics,
Mathematics and the knowledge of Nature—which played a
principal part in Thomist wisdom, because it was drawn
from the essential diversity of objects` to be known (*orders
of abstraction*)—and which witnessed the domination of the
object over our minds. One single Science—which logically
implies a single and identical degree of abstraction and of in-

telligibility for everything that we can know. All the disciplines of the intellect henceforth are to be stretched out upon a same level of intelligibility, they will depend essentially upon the same light, they will require necessarily the same kind of certitude, they will of necessity make use of the same method, varied in its applications, one in its essence: the SCIENTIFIC METHOD, that keen, levelling sovereign, refuge and comforter of the modern world, that has made such headway since the *Discourse*.[58]

The sciences, according to the ancients, were the laborious work of an intellect that drew its ideas of things through the senses, immaterializing by abstraction the objects it attracted to itself, and by that very fact subject to discursive movement, to all the difficulties and all the precautions of logic; the work of an intellect which was to begin *tabula rasa,* and which received from tangible realities everything except its nature and its spiritual light. Science thus conceived built itself up on strict dependence upon things, and could regulate its exigencies only upon those of the object. Cartesian Science, on the contrary, is the work of an intellect which finds within itself, innate, all the ideas it needs, and which as a result is directly dependent upon, and receives everything from, God Who created it and not from the things it knows; the clear view of *simple natures* and of their connections, the notion of which is imprinted by God upon the soul from birth, is the instrument of our reason, more intuitive than discursive to the philosopher's taste. Science thus conceived is constructed within the mind without suffering the contact and domination of things, with which doubtless it is finally in agreement, but only by reason of the play of exigencies of the mind itself, and thanks to the veracity of Him Who made both things and mind.

That idea of science, only too flattering to our tendency to delight in our acquired knowledge, and to domineer over the real, will take on singular developments in the philosophers' speculations as well as in the use made of science at certain times. Finally, human thought will appear as a sort of demi-god fabricating the cognoscible world with its concepts; and it is not reality which will require science to be true, it is Science that will require reality to be "scientific," and to produce its credentials.

But to possess such a science, all of whose elements are born with our mind, and which is thus only an orderly unfolding of ourselves or our thought, do we need to have certain qualities come forth to perfect our faculty of knowing? Descartes, in rejecting the accidents and qualities as fiction, suppresses in a general way those habitus and virtues that gave Thomist psychology the means of a subtle and profound realism that modern psychology has scarcely rediscovered. In particular it destroys the intellectual habitus, and the real meaning of its doctrine is that "common sense" or "natural light,"—reason just as we receive it from nature and not as it is fashioned by the teaching of masters (worthy of the name—they were hardly that any more) and especially by the intercourse with objects difficult to grapple with, *reason in the state of nature* is fitted to arrive, from the instant it makes use of the Method, at the summits of science and of wisdom. A claim for unculturedness to which was given, from then on, some satisfaction.

One consequence of that suppression of the intellectual

habitus is that the idea of science inevitably becomes purely material: science is no longer a spiritual quality within us, a light, a living fire which intrinsically perfects our soul, it is nothing but a collection of well-ordered concepts in us, that "accumulation," that "co-ordination of notions"[59] where the ancients used to see only the material of science, and which they carefully distinguished from intellectual virtue itself—the "interior force." From then on, the true notion of the growth of science in the mind was to disappear, whether it was a question of the "intensive growth," which happens when the mind "penetrates the same truth in a more profound and vehement fashion, and clings to it more strongly,"[60] or of the "extensive growth" properly so-called, which takes place when the inner force that constitutes the habitus dilates and rises up to attain new conclusions and new objects. Science does not increase except by extrinsic addition, like a heap piling up and spreading out, so that by a consequence which Descartes certainly did not foresee (for he was a great enemy of erudition) Science born of his reform—I mean to say the idea that was to be created of Science—could, by confusing the true progressive movement of science with the research of vast merely material increments, only crush and weaken the mind as a fire one smothers with too much fuel.

More generally, the suppression of intellectual habitus will cause us little by little to lose sight of the fact that science is something of a determined subject, something of man, the intrinsic perfecting of a being endowed with a certain nature and situated in certain conditions; the tendency is more and more to look upon it as an absolute which is sufficient to itself in the abstract, and which sits enthroned in the ideological heavens:

science which is neither astronomy nor botany, which is not human science or angelic science or divine science, which is THE SCIENCE.

This Science perfectly one has a single kind of light and a single kind of certitude. What light and what certitude? Those which are peculiar to mathematics, since in mathematics alone does Descartes find, or think he finds, the pure type both of those innate and self-evident ideas which in his eyes are the *semina scientiae,* and of those series of coupled evidences to which he reduces reasoning. Is the Science it is his mission to make known to the world anything other than a universalized mathematics? Here is where the philosophy of clear ideas comes in, and that need for universal apparent clarity, which will banish from the world authorized by Science, all reality involving for us obscurity or mystery; and will, to speak truth, render all sound metaphysics of divine transcendance absolutely impossible to the heirs of Descartes.

St. Thomas observes that of all the sciences mathematics is the one best fitted to our mind; its object is, in effect, more intelligible *in itself* than that of the sciences of nature, too over-shadowed as it is by matter and situated in the lowest degree of abstraction; and it is more intelligible *for us* than that of meta-physics, too purely immaterial and too highly abstract. A wisdom of mathematical order is not then to be, as Aristotle avers metaphysical wisdom is, too divine a good which we can enjoy only by precarious right and which is loaned to us rather than given; it is to be possessed by us in full ownership—a wisdom to our own measure. Furthermore, it is to be an easy wisdom—not that mathematics is easy, for all science is difficult—

but in the sense that mathematics among the great intellectual disciplines is the easiest for man (we have child prodigies in mathematics, but not in the other sciences). Nay more, if the intellectual habitus are suppressed, those habitus whose function it is to raise our intelligence to the height of the object and to make of it an aristocrat, it is because it is easy for everyone to learn science by means of a good method.

It is thus that Descartes was promising to make "even those who have never studied" arrive at "the very secrets of the most curious sciences." Ignorance is not due to a "lack of mind" or to a "lack of skill"; *"there is nothing, in general, that another man can know, that he"* who possesses the key to clear ideas and practices the true method *"is not, himself, capable of knowing, provided that he applies his mind to it suitably."*[61] Science is for everyone. Clear ideas are, in practice, easy ideas; metaphysically conceived as pure flashes of the constitutive light of our mind, and poured into us by the Creator with our being, "easy" then in the beginning like ideas of angels, in the end they will be, in fact, merely ideas easy to handle, "easy" as the mental pictures of a piece of machinery to assemble: reason more and more disintellectualized, and without being conscious of it, invaded by imagination and spatiality; rationalism is, if one may put it so, the *intellectualism of the imagination.* And if Science necessitates fighting battles and requires constant hard work, it is in order that obstacles raised by prejudice may be overcome, that the world of illusions may be swept away, that world which rises from the mists of a long infancy, and whose awakening reason still remembers. Method has as its function precisely to thrust aside obstacles (*removere prohibentia*). Reason in travail is no longer an intrinsically feeble creature that forms and builds up its own organism by a patient life-giving labor—it is a young god, in shackles, who shakes off his bonds. With regard to this reason, to its nature and its innate power, Science is, in itself, easy.[62]

Not only is it for everyone, but also it has rights over everything. In the conceptions of Aristotle and of St. Thomas, our science doubtless bears on the whole extent of the real, in the sense that in every reality it can find where to come to grips, but, because it proceeds by abstraction, its knowledge attains in everything only zones of sufficiently high and, so-to-speak, distilled intelligibility, and in that sense one may say that only one part of the real—the essential laws of being and of abstract natures or their experimental substitutes—can be for us an object of science, that is to say, of demonstrative certitude; there are some things which are not the object of human science. Wherever intelligible necessity does not reign, wherever it is impossible to resolve a conclusion into necessary reasons for being, that is to say, in the huge domain of liberty, of contingency, of the singular taken as such, science must give place to opinion, to belief, to probability, or to simple certitudes of fact. Furthermore the sciences themselves, being sciences of man, and arduous victories won over the uncertain, comprise a large portion of simple probable, a portion all the larger, and the less reducible as these sciences are closer to matter and to individual particularities. And their very certitudes emerge, if I may say so, from probable knowledge; they separate after slow elaboration, for they are the outcome of a progressive movement—the absolute stabilization of the scientific *judicium* completing normally a process of *invention* or of discovery which, in itself, reaches the truth only in a fluctuating or opinionative manner.

Descartes, on the contrary, who with the rest of the moderns makes science consist in invention rather than in judgment, has a hankering for a Science which with one and the same movement proves by discovering, and discovers by proving, established in complete certitude from its inception, rejecting of itself as an attempt against its being, every purely probable element. "Never-less, I wish them to think that if what I have written about that (the movement of the heart and the circulation of the blood), or about refractions, or about any other matter I may have dealt with in more than three lines in what I have had printed—if that prove false, all the rest of my Philosophy is worthless."[63] And he professes to boot that outside the practical field where the necessities of action force us to choose, everything that is solely opinon, all that is not established or justified by Science can without inconvenience be taken as false—in other words, does not exist for the understanding:[64] Science, that one and indivisible science, infrangible, adamantine, all certitude and purely knowledge, perfect Word engendered by Thought, free from the servitude of infancy, then, is going to claim rights over the whole being. It is in the singular as such that the intellectualist nominalism of the new philosophy will proceed; it will demand scientific knowledge of every detail of events in the concatenation of their becoming, its universality will thus become quantitative and material; and with the exact and fruitful idea of a science "of the nature of things," or, on the experimental plane, of a science *of the laws of nature,* will come to join the parasitic idea of a science which seizes hold on and can foresee in some supreme equation *the course of nature* in the infinite detail of its concrete unfolding. On the other hand we shall see all sorts of disciplines turned toward the singular or toward the practical, and closer to art than to science, we shall see History itself, which Descartes scorned so supremely, become *science*—to the detriment of their own nature—in order to have the right to exist.

Finally, Science by itself constitutes the happiness of men. It sets them free, sufficing fully unto themselves.[65] Let it so much as establish its reign and we shall see "to what degree of Wisdom, to what perfection of life, to what bliss"[66] humanity will find its way. And it is an affair of two or three centuries. There is an earthly bliss—relative, doubtless, but incomparably superior to our present condition—which it rests with Science to procure for us.

The pride of human knowledge appears thus as the very substance, solid and resistant, of rationalist hopes. Pride, a dense pride without frivolity or distraction, as stable as virtue, as vast as geometric extension, bitter and restless as the ocean, takes possession of Descartes to such an extent that it would seem the universal form of his interior workings and the principle of all his suffering. We know what bitter, dark envy he fostered against Aristotle, and what torment he suffered at still not having supplanted him in the schools. Did he not feel obliged to give to humanity a definitive and unshakable "full body of philosophy"? There was not even the question of old age and death over which he had not thought for some time to triumph.[67] Today, taught by many experiences and disappointments, we can scarcely imagine to what degree of presumption and of swaggering fever, to what heights of self-confidence reason was rising at the dawn of the classical era. A little longer and it will know everything.

> One of the very unity of understanding,
> > spring, from God in us, not from things,
> > born of a pure unfolding of Thought in the absolute,
> > universally bathed in mathematical clarity, easy for reason,
> > everywhere certain and made to exhaust reality,
> > beatific,

all these essentially mythical characteristics glitter on the Science-idol of our forefathers. In the thought of Descartes that idol is not, doubtless, drawn full-length, clothed in all its clear attributes; it appears nevertheless, virtually pre-formed like a sparkling spiritual germ passing and repassing in the background of the system, and having been present from the beginning. If we endeavor intellectually to revive the doctrine of Descartes to catch up his original intuitions, if we are careful to follow the directions in his text, to grasp the internal logic of his principles, to bring the consequences developed in the course of history closer to the formal data legible in the beginning, we must conclude, I believe, that the *Myth of Science* is the very token of the mind of Descartes, and the first gift he gave us.

CHAPTER III

THE DEPOSITION OF WISDOM

CHAPTER III

DEPOSITION OF WISDOM

Descartes not only distorted the concept of science—and for how many centuries? but at the same time he destroyed the foremost and most immaterial of human hierarchies, the order of intellectual disciplines.

As Mr. Henry Gouhier has correctly pointed out, the solutions traditionally given to the problem of the relations between reason and faith, and between philosophy and theology, form a part of the material that Descartes received ready-made from the knowledge of his time, material on which he personally reflects as little as possible, and which he exploits extensively in his replies to his adversaries. The formulas he uses, when questioned on this subject, seem to be simple repetitions of the formulas current among the Scholastic theologians. So much so in fact, that certain subtle minds have been taken in by it; doubtless they have been perfectly well aware of the difference in spiritual orientation which distinguishes Descartes from St. Thomas—but they have not understood that this difference is of an absolutely formal order, resting as it does on something quite different from subjective dispositions: so they have accepted as identical the Cartesian and the Thomist positions on this question of faith and theology in their relation to reason and philosophy. This at any rate provides a rather convenient way of satisfying at little cost the distrust they harbor with respect to the Angelic Doctor.

In reality, Descartes was the victim, on this and on many other points, of his fixed determination not to probe certain questions, either on account of their danger or because they had no immediate connection with his scientific interests. This determination was as expeditious as it was useful, and a very prudent one too, one we cannot help comparing with those precautions of shrewdest policy we sometimes take with regard to ourselves in the interest of some over-ruling passion, be it even the passion of philosophy. The result is that in repeating the formulas, and under the impression that he is reproducing the classical doctrine of the theologians, he unconsciously injects a meaning which is quite different. Briefly, he realizes in a *material* way—and thereby falsifies—the conception of faith and theology of the ancients.

DESCARTES AND FAITH

With regard to faith, it is true that he affirms (in replying to the Second Objections, in a manner conforming with the purest traditional doctrine[70]—for he is obviously very pleased at this point to display his knowledge *in divinis*), it is true that he affirms that faith has as its "formal reason" "a certain inner light with which God has supernaturally enlightened us, and from which we obtain an assured confidence that the things which are propounded for us to believe have been revealed by Him, and that it is quite impossible for Him to be guilty of falsehood and to deceive us."

But if he thus gives the *lumen fidei* and the intellect their place as far as the formal motive of faith is concerned, does he admit that in its very substance the act of faith, although directed by the will, is still an act of the speculative intellect, adhering to a datum which is obscure, but with the unquenchable desire to *see* and to penetrate within? He cannot admit it; his general theory of judgment prevents him. Is it not well known, that he takes from the intellect the function of judging (which was precisely its perfection in the eyes of the ancients), in order to ascribe this function completely to the domain of the will? This voluntaristic doctrine which is already a pretty monstrosity in philosophy, is accompanied by the gravest consequences for the theory of faith.

Let us glance at the Thomist analysis of the act of faith. The act of faith, the act of adhering or assenting to the revealed truth, in affirming *"ita est,* thus it is, not because I see it, but because God has said it"* is, for St. Thomas, an act of the intellect, an act produced or "elicited" by the intellect, though it be by the determinative action of the will (moved by grace), and not by the action of the object itself, which is non-evident; consequently the intellect of the one who has the faith, while adhering with an absolute certitude to the revealed object, and remaining fixed to it by an unshakable assent, continues to seek and to struggle to acquire better knowledge of it. It enjoys certitude, but it does not enjoy the vision, it is secure, but it is not satisfied: *motus intellectus nondum est quietatus, sed adhuc habet cogitationem et inquisitionem de his quae credit, quamvis firmissime eis assenti-at: quantum enim est ex seipso, non est ei satisfactum . . .*[71] Thus it is that the intellect is spoken of as *held captive by* faith because it is fixed there as from without, and not by its own intrinsic good, which is the evidence of the object; a captivity which delivers and which sets at ease, *expedit,*[72] because it causes adherence to God.

Faith therefore (opposed not to *knowledge* as in Kant, but to knowledge by *vision* and to *science* properly speaking, that is, to knowledge in the perfect mode), faith then is an imperfect knowledge according to the mode of knowing[73] (since it is founded wholly on the testimony of God, not on the evidence of the object itself), but is a real knowledge,[74] and superior to all human knowledge by its infallible certitude as well as by its object, which is God attained according to His own very essence. By that faith it is given to us to enter into participation with the divine understanding, *intellegere divinum*,[75] and to consider all things as if with the eyes of God—*quasi oculo dei*.[76] And so it tends toward evidence and being face-to-face with God as a movement tends toward its end; it involves essentially a *movement toward vision: fides importat motum quemdam intellectus ad visionem in qua quietatur, fides requirit visionem gloriae, tanquam terminus status viae*.[77] That is why the intellect, uplifted by faith to the divine truth, demands to be completed still further by the gifts of intelligence and wisdom, and becomes the disciple of love, to give us a foretaste of the truth it knows, but which it cannot here below devour by vision.

In Descartes, on the contrary, the very act of adherence to the revealed datum becomes—being a judgment: *ita est*—an act elicited by the will. "Faith appertains to the will."[78] Now, the will is in fact a blind faculty; how could it have the desire to see? Having accomplished that act of assent—to an obscure object, it must be added, therefore deprived of interest for an understanding which has its perfection only in clear ideas—the will has nothing further to seek, it stops, it rests. It is at its end. This explains the "static" aspect in the faith of Descartes, which

Mr. Laberthonnière[79] has drawn attention to; it is a materialized faith, a satisfied faith which is content to obey and does not seek to know; *fides NON quaerens intellectum* . . . One might say that Descartes sticks to the formulas of faith without concerning himself further with grasping the truths they contain. Nay, he clings to them the more surely and the more respectfully the less he bothers about grasping their truth. From this point of view let us judge the real significance of his famous declaration: "I have never dealt with the Infinite save to submit myself to it," and his firm resolution to be and to remain "of the religion of his king and of his foster-mother."

> *O crystalline fountain,*
> *If only in your silvery reflections*
> *You would suddenly allow to appear*
> *The ever-to-be desired Eyes*
> *Which I carry outlined in my heart!*

St. John of the Cross,[80] designating the propositions or articles of faith by "silvery reflections," "relative to the gold which is the substance of Faith, or the truths it contains considered in themselves,"[81] St. John of the Cross lives only to see the eyes of God, those eyes so ardently desired, of which divine faith is a sketch within his heart. As for Descartes, he is satisfied with the "silvery reflections," he needs only the surface of the fountain. One may ask oneself which, the philosopher or the mystic, is in this case the most truly *intellectual* . . .

Descartes' faith is indeed a supernatural certitude that opens to us the possibility of achieving heaven. But is it *from this moment and from here below* a beginning of life eternal, *quaedam inchoatio vitae aeternae,* which "consists in the full knowledge of God"?[82] Not at all! Cartesian thought, here as elsewhere, separates and disassociates, isolates; no longer is there any connection between heaven and the baptised earth, between eternal life and human life. Faith as Descartes conceives it is not a growing force, which in growing supernaturalizes the whole soul, and which has its full development only in the fully-supernaturalized soul; it is encysted within the soul.

I do not cast doubts upon the sincerity of Descartes' faith, a sincerity which to my mind is not in question.

With his very lofty sense of order and authority in the world and in the state, Descartes would have a horror of "rationalism" in religious matters; for him religion is the foundation and the guarantee of human order, as divine truth is of human knowledge; he rests his philosophy upon the unfathomable infinity of God; he holds firmly to his faith, and dies a good Catholic. Descartes was sincerely Catholic; I think everyone is in accord on that point today.[83] One may however be allowed to observe that many diverse states of mind, and of a greater or less degree of integrity, can find themselves compatible with *sincerity.* In Descartes' time—a period much less homogeneous and much less disciplined than one might ordinarily imagine—what strange and discordant elements blended, in many people, with a sincere Catholic faith?[84] While detesting atheists and libertines, and defending Religion, one might in one case be a Stoic, in another a Skeptic, here an Epicurean, and there a Platonist, and soon it will be a case of Jansenism . . . To tell the truth Descartes has at once something of the Platonists and something of the Stoics

66

of his century—of the first in the speculative order, of the second in the practical order. Everything leads one to think that his religion was very close to the rather special Christianity common among the Neo-Stoics, which, confining faith and the supernatural gifts of grace to the precisely-defined domain of the *moral virtue of religion,* and the obligations of worship, was in every other case seeking *its* principles of conduct in reason alone. When Descartes, in anticipation of the time when he would have recast human knowledge, and built up the scientific ethics, wishes to decide upon his rules of action, does he think of the simple ethics which suffices for the faithful and whose precepts are there, ready to hand? No, he asks his reason to construct for him a provisional ethics . . .

Among men who are as great "lovers of liberty"[85] as Descartes, such a Christianity, outside of the limited domain just referred to, provides a clear field in every direction; one might say a sort of agreement concluded between Grace and Nature, in order at once to gain heaven by Religion and earth by Reason. We have here from a certain point of view, a kind of displacement of humility, that is, according to this conception, the humility of the layman seems to consist in *putting in a place apart* the things of religion (is that not the portion reserved for the clergy?) and being exclusively *submissive to,* mechanically submissive to the Church, but without receiving of her life— *Domine non sum dignus;* and are we here so very far from the point of view expressed in Arnauld's *De la fréquente communion?*[86] Then from another point of view, not exclusive of the first moreover, Descartes' religion seems like a simple insurance taken against the risks of the beyond, which should leave him free here below to conduct his life, his philosophy and his pleasures as his reason alone dictates. All that in no way prevents that faith from being sincere. But it is the sign that this sincere faith has been seriously immobilized, in a water-tight compartment. Thanks to a happy and sagacious division of labor which the Gospel had not foreseen, one can serve two masters at the same time, drawing nothing but profit from the one without losing any of the benefits promised by the other.

In regard particularly to the work of reason, Descartes could indeed take credit for apologetic aims, although Mr. Espinas has greatly over-stated this point and the judgment of Mr. Gilson still remains exact: "As for the Church, Descartes respected her and, more especially, feared her deeply; and being much less careful to defend her than preoccupied with defending himself against her, he sought above all to conciliate her": briefly, "he devoted himself only to his own cause." Descartes, furthermore, because he has recourse to expeditious methods, and does not take the trouble to give his doctrine sufficient rational elaboration, and because on the other hand he is imbued with Christian *habits*—can allow many elements borrowed from things religious to filter into his philosophy. Faith, however, can never play that powerful part of superior orientation, of *stella rectrix*[87] with regard to his reason, which certainly does not suppose in the soul the least confusion between the rational and the revealed, but supposes rather a vital and luminous influence from the heaven of theological virtues upon the natural virtues of the intellect.[88]

Thus, whether it is a question of his manner of living the

faith, or his conception of it, the author of the *Discourse on Method* appears, in spite of superficial analogies, as though animated with a spirit fundamentally different from the spirit of St. Thomas. The thought of the one is in this case like a materialized diminution, a mechanization of the thought of the other.

DESCARTES AND THEOLOGY

The same thing holds good for theology. Looking at the surface of things, one might think that Descartes retained purely and simply the traditional notion of theology he had received from his masters at La Flèche. And he thought so himself; for the Scholastics as for him, is not the theologian he who rationally deals with and develops the revealed dogmas?

Let us meanwhile ask the thelogians to tell us what they think of theology.[89] For St. Thomas theology, which is a true science and a science essentially superior to philosophy because it owes its principles—by means of faith—to the very knowledge of God and the blessèd, the very perfect evidence of which is infinitely above all our natural evidence, and to which theology is subordinated—theology implies a *habitus* or an internal virtue of knowledge and judgment in the intellect, let us say a "light"[90] distinct from and superior to that of philosophy: the light of reason *illuminated and perfected by faith*. Supernatural faith indeed is to theology what the intelligence of principles is to the sciences of the natural order, and the theological *habitus* is acquired with its assistance and under its sway, in such a way that if the theologian loses this infused faith he loses theological *science*—he can retain materially all its notions, and so to speak,

its corpse; he no longer possesses it as science. In other words
this science, even though it is a formally natural intellectual
virtue like mathematics or philosophy, is nevertheless supernatural in its root, *radicaliter et virtualiter;* from which it follows
that in theology reason illuminated by faith is also strengthened
by it,[91] if not with regard to its mode of procedure, which
remains our natural discursive mode with all its imperfections,
at least with regard to its superior certitude, to its superior
penetration and the superior power of discernment for which
it is indebted to the height of the supernaturally believed principles into which it resolves its conclusions. Theology is derived
from the light of natural principles, "seed of all the sciences
of the natural order," only in so far as these principles "are
enlightened and perfected by the light of faith,"[92] it judges,
approves, defends and explains in the light of its own principles
the conclusions and principles of the sciences which it makes
use of, and confers upon them a higher certitude—even upon
the first principles, such as the principle of contradiction.[93]
That is what gives us an idea of the true nature of this science,
considered not, perhaps, such as it is in a great number of theolo-
gizing minds, but such as it is in its pure essence, and as a Thomas
Aquinas lived it. As a man who is subject to the labors and
difficulties of discourse and to the inferiority of the human mode
of proceeding, but uplifted by infused faith to a knowledge of
things divine, the theologian, humble and magnanimous, believes
without seeing—like the smallest of the *parvuli* beloved of our
Lord—the truths which are the principles of his wisdom; and
deducing with all the force of demonstration, that which is virtually contained in these truths, he bears in the fragile vessel of

his mind-of-man a knowledge more certain in itself than any human knowledge . . .

If then theology, although in itself, *ratione sui ipsius* independent of every philosophical system, must nevertheless make use of philosophy *ratione subjecti,* because of the weakness of the human subject in which it is developing, it does indeed use philosophy as an instrument which it subordinates to itself, judging by its own light, and assuming among all the philosophical doctrines the one it judges to be in its hands and the best instrument of truth for its own ends.

Now, what becomes of all that in Descartes? In his eyes there are no accidents, or qualities, either habitus or virtues, which inwardly bring to higher perfection the intellectual faculty and its natural light; which, as we have seen, constitutes the unity of Science.

Consequently faith cannot co-operate in the acquisition, by exercise and by study, of a special scientific habitus, or of a discretive and judicative virtue "added" to the understanding. Theology, if it be not a question of revelation or of prophetic inspiration, if it does not call for some "extraordinary assistance from heaven," as the philosopher pretends to suppose when with ceremonious impertinence he refers to theologians as being "more than men" ("plus qu'hommes")—theology can only derive *as science* from our natural light considered *as unperfectible* by any superadded intrinsic quality, and therefore taken *as purely natural.* As a matter of fact, in prohibiting the natural light from perfecting itself by any superadded quality whatsoever, in speaking of "natural" light *in opposition to habitus,* Descartes thereby forbids this natural light to acquire any superadded perfecting, natural in itself and supernatural in its origin, such as the theological habitus. His expression "natural" light must be understood *in opposition to the original or root supernaturality* which St. Thomas attributes to the theological habitus. For Descartes, *if theology is a science* as St. Thomas claimed, it is dependent upon the same *light of knowledge* as philosophy; in short, it is nothing more than a simple *application of philosophy* to the revealed datum, and properly speaking, a science subordinated to philosophy. (And in fact he does regard Scholastic theology as subordinated to the philosophy of Aristotle.) It is thus that the notion of theology which he had received from the ancients becomes purely material in his thought.

But after all, is this such a serious fault, and do not certain theologians seem to think like Descartes on this point? In reality, for anyone who regards the matter from the standpoint of principles, what it amounts to is the very destruction of theology. For there should be proportion between the proposed object and the subjective power—that interior virtue which causes judgment; and if in order to establish a rational conclusion bearing on a divine object we make use of a power of deduction which is itself not rooted in supernatural faith, we shall not have a knowledge but a misunderstanding of that object. To say that theology is *philosophy applied to revealed truth* is to say by definition that theology is the scientific misunderstanding of revealed truth (in the same way that a certain exegesis which, deprived of the theological habitus, is nothing more than the purely rational light—"animal" in St. Paul's meaning of the word—of historical criticism applied to the word of God). Descartes himself did not fail to perceive this consequence: and therein lies one of the reasons for his final inclination to refuse to admit of theology as a science.

Let us look meanwhile at the logical effects of the principle affirmed.

How could philosophy rightly be submitted to the extrinsic and negative control of a theology which claims to be a science when it is only an application of philosophy to a divine datum, and does not have within itself its own light as a superior science? Actually there will be many points at which they touch: but these will be between two disciplines which, by a singular illogicality (though they bear upon objects of a very unequal nature), can be considered equal as regards their science value, which springs wholly from pure reason. The philosopher and the theologian can henceforth be considered merely as two specialists working in different domains: the idea of a specialization on the same plane thus replacing the notion of a hierarchical subordination. And of a certainty, truth cannot be different in theology from what it is in philosophy;[05] but if it happens that the philosopher and the theologian meet, the theologian can after all give notice to the philosopher that a certain purely philosophical proposition has a certain unfortunate consequence in his special and (at least in regard to the social authority he enjoys) privileged domain; he cannot *judge* as a theologian that this purely philosophical proposition is false. And above all, such points of contact are simple meetings of a material order, accidental clashes, which it is wise to render as infrequent as possible, because being pure extrinsic restraints which it is necessary to submit to, but which do not enlighten, they are contrary to the free development of philosophy.

Philosophy will therefore tend to dissociate itself from theology, and to seek its own better-being in shutting itself off from it. The theological atmosphere in which Descartes works, the presence of numerous theological materials in his doctrine should not hide from us that essential aspect of the Cartesian reform which we have doubtless made explicit here, but of which Descartes himself was certainly and clearly aware.

*

*   *

These are however, only the immediate consequences of the deterioration that the notion of theology suffers in Descartes' thought; other consequences will follow.

Let us briefly enunciate these logical derivations: first of all, philosophy, pursuing to the very end that tendency toward isolation revealed in Descartes himself, will reach the point where it absolutely rejects the control of theology, as being a violence imposed upon its nature as a discipline of evident principles; it will no longer be merely *distinct* from theology, as the Schoolmen taught it, it will *separate* itself completely from theology (as later the State separated itself from the Church), go to work on its own, completely ignoring theology, and claim the right to its own perfect autonomy.

But more than that, philosophy, that is to say Science, *the* Science, one of the very unity of the understanding, will become the one and only Science: how could there be room for another science in addition to *the* Science? How could another science be possible where there is but one single light of science, of which philosophy is already the work?

It will be sufficient, moreover, to analyze the notion of science as Descartes introduced it, in order to understand what insoluble difficulties are henceforth to beset theology considered as a science. Theology has only one instrument of rational progress and of extension of scientific certitude: syllogistic deduction. For Descartes, the syllogism is an empty tautology, and should give way to a kind of synthetic intuition of two terms which he still calls deduction; mathematical reasoning, he thinks, provides the type of such deduction, but it would certainly be of no use in theology where we do not work on "simple natures." Above all, theology has as its object something properly divine, hence *obscure* to the gaze of every created mind, that is: the mystery of the Deity, which no idea can comprehend. For Descartes however, what constitutes science is that it has for its object *ideas evident in themselves* (clear ideas, simple natures) or else a reality reducible by analysis to such ideas. Let us understand this point well. The ancients also looked upon evidence as a condition of science. But that evidence, the foundation of the certitude essential to science, was to them the evidence of the *propositions* or of the *objects of judgment* which constitute the principles of science, and which in a science *subordinated* to another—as perspective is to geometry, or theology to the science of God and the blessed—are no doubt inevident to the sub-ordinated science, but are evident to the subordinating science; this is sufficient to assure the subordinated science (even in a subject which does not see, but believes its principles) if not the perfect state of science at least the certitude proper to it.[96] That the thing itself attained might in itself be superior to our intelligence and therefore imperfectly intelligible for us, should in no way hinder us—thanks to the revelation of the principles—

from thus acquiring the science of it. For an object too luminous for our mind remains capable of attainment by an idea inadequate (non-quidditative, analogical), but nevertheless veracious.* That is how the Mediaevals were able to study the mysteries scientifically and to arrive, as "at the summit of supreme humility," at the sacred science of God.

This science is authentically *science,* although in virtue of the subject in which it is found, it may not be in a completely scientific state.** It will only enjoy that state when it is continued with the vision. Thus the supreme science, which is pre-adapted to divine conditions and not commensurate in itself with the dimensions of our understanding, is summoned, in so far as it is science, to a better state,[97] and is itself intrinsically submitted to the anagogical law on which the life of the soul depends.

Descartes' position is entirely different. The evidence required by science is for him the evidence of the *ideas,* of the *objects of notion* which constitute at the same time the principles and the matter of science. Consequently, if the thing itself attained is not evident for us, clearly and distinctly intelligible for us, or reducible to something evident for us, it cannot by any right be an object of science. *Adjusting* everything *to the level of reason,*[98] that is to say (for one should take the word 'reason' in its most formal sense), to the level of *human* intelligence and of *human* ideas, the philosophy of clear ideas not only excludes the whole vast infrarational world of "mystery," which

---

* We can thus acquire, *by the grace of God, some intelligence of the mysteries, and a very fruitful intelligence,* without however succeeding in *seeing them after the manner of the truths which constitute the object proper of our reason.* (Definition of the Council of the Vatican, see note 101.)

** *Proprie et substantialiter scientia, licet sub statu imperfecto.* Cf. John of St. Thomas, *Curs. theol.,* in I, P.q. 1, disp. 2, a.3; ed. of Solesmes, vol. I, p. 353.

matter, individuality and contingence cause to subsist in the natural order, not only does it reject from things any residue obscure in itself and too lacking in being for the intellect to grasp—but furthermore it is essentially repugnant to the idea of supra-rational mystery, of divine mystery, as the object of a *science* made possible by revelation.

Is this the explanation of how Descartes, with respect to his personal preoccupations, can maintain such a tranquil indifference with regard to theology? Is it because, as a practical man, he is, in religion, interested only in the business of his salvation, and because "the most simple-minded can succeed therein as well as the most intelligent," the road to heaven being "no less open to the most ignorant than to the most learned"? Possibly, but it is too easy to reply that even in the interests of their salvation the *majores in Ecclesia* should be more learned than others in the things of faith. In reality, what governs his attitude is the idea that theology, as he told Burman, *is better the simpler it is,* that theology is better in the "simpleton" than in the "scholar," in short, that it is a matter of common sense, not of science, and that after all faith is sufficient. To refuse to allow theology to be a science is, moreover, the sole means of preventing it from being subordinated to philosophy.[99] Here we have the heart of the matter, the inner core of Descartes' opinions with regard to theology. Not only must it be said that the traditional conception of theology became more material in him, as we indicated above, so that for him theology, *if* it is a science and *to the extent* that it is a science, is no more than an application of philosophy to revealed data; but one must add that realizing the disadvantages and the dangers—both for the dignity of revealed faith and for the security of philosophers—of such a conception of theology, he tried to eliminate it by denying that theology was a science, by denying the existence and the possibility of a theological *science*.

This idea, it seems to me, was present in his mind from the beginning, from the time of the *Discourse on Method,* but latently, implicitly, like a practical attitude rather than as a theoretical conviction; and not being clearly set forth, it did not prevent Descartes—yielding on another plane of thought, as though to a sort of routine, to attitudes of mind acquired at school and current among the public—from having had recourse himself to the notion of a theological science.* This idea must have taken clearer shape as time went on—and as a result of his experience with the disillusionments suffered at the hands of the theologians. In any case it is indeed the fundamental and truly personal idea of Descartes; it is the idea he reveals to Burman two years before his death, in an intimate conversation where he relaxes somewhat from his ordinary precautions: it no doubt pertains to reason to "prove that the truth of faith are not opposed to philosophical truths,"[100] and do not contain impossibilities, but it should be limited to this purely negative duty; our understanding could not penetrate into the very truths of faith *in any way—non debemus eas ullo modo examinare*—the crime of Scholasticism was precisely to wish to examine them; their interconnection, from the very fact that they are revealed, escapes our intelligence—*nos earum veritatum nexum ita consequi et intellegere non possumus, quia a revelatione dependent.*[101] A state of mind shared more or less consciously it seems,

* See note 109.

by a certain number of hurried Christians who do not suspect the dangers it entails for faith itself.

What then is the hidden root of this anti-theological fideism in Descartes? It is that faith itself, which supplies theology with all its principles, is now no longer opposed only to *science* in the sense that the same object cannot be *seen* and at the same time *believed*, an object of science and an object of faith. Faith tends, at least virtually and in practice, to be opposed to *cognition*, to cease to be a cognition and to become a simple submission of the will, a simple obedience to authority, obedience to God considered as absolute Authority, not as primary Truth. Because all things considered, the objects it offers us, being characterized as essentially obscure, are not only inevident and *imperfectly intelligible* to us, they are in themselves *absolutely inaccessible* to our minds, *absolutely unintelligible* to us, they are beyond our power of knowing. It is strange to see the earliest signs of a misconception come to light in Descartes, which, fostered in Protestant soil, will become in Kant the famous opposition between "faith" and "knowledge."

Descartes thought to safeguard faith by isolating it from intelligence, by making a discrimination at once simple, radical, expeditious and particularly adapted to his personal convenience, between the *clear,* object of science, and the *obscure,* which can be object of revelation (for our finite understanding cannot impose its limits upon the Creator). He thought to safeguard faith by making both the human domain of science and the divine domain of revelation appendant to the incomprehensible and infinite omnipotence of the God Who can neither err nor cause to err. But he kept them two absolutely disconnected domains having no contact one with the other, in such a way as to put the divine realm *wholly and completely* out of reach of our understanding.

He did not perceive that he was succeeding only too well with his enterprise. He has so much respect for revealed datum that he does not dare even to apply his intelligence to it; he places the things of God so carefully beyond the reach of our mind that it can henceforth understand nothing about them; in order the better to worship God, he raises the Cross so high that it becomes invisible. It is a case of too much respect, too much fear: as though the union of reason with infused faith could only bring about disasters, and as though our understanding was *absolutely* incapable, even with grace and faith, of arriving at *some intelligence* of the depth of God. There, in its pure formal line, is the most characteristic tendency of Cartesian thought, irrespective of the attenuations and the deflections which it may have undergone at the hands of the philosopher in virtue of his subjective inclinations. That is why Mr. Maurice Blondel was able to speak of "Christian agnosticism" with regard to Descartes.[102] The separation is too perfect and the solution is only too obviously a provisional one, this friendly estrangement being bound, by the very nature of things, to turn to conflict. Henceforth between reason and mystery, between science and faith, the antinomy is inevitable.

It is in this respect especially that the spirit of Descartes, considered as the animating form of modern thought, appears as the spirit of rationalism properly so called. In Descartes himself it is manifested by practical attitudes and deep-seated tendencies, rather than by a systematic ideology, and it continues to be governed by the traditional heritage. In Descartes' successors it will parade itself in the full light of day. As a result of its interference with extraneous elements, and in virtue of the particular combinations of the historical moment in which it happened to be operating, the spirit of rationalism gave rise to all sorts of various forms: theological reaction, but absorption of theology into philosophy, in Malebranche; exegetic rationalism among the Protestant theologians of the Low Countries; religious criticism among the English deists. Left to itself this spirit tended (logically and inexorably) to this final stage (expressed at the very outset in the rigid thought of Spinoza): "The aim of philosophy is nothing other than truth; that of faith, nothing but obedience and piety. *Philosophiae scopus nihil est praeter veritatem; Fidei autem, nihil praeter obedientiam et pietatem;*"[103] and consequently theology, if it is not reduced to philosophy itself, is only an exercise of ignoramuses chattering about the unknown, or at best, an arrangement of formulas quite practical in scope, indicating to the faithful the moral attitude and rules of action which they should adopt, *rationem et modum obediendi;*[104] a conception which, combined with the idealistic philosophy of the nineteenth century,[105] was later to work strangely widespread destruction.

The work of Descartes, whatever may have been the intentions of the author, comes to this, finally, that it not only separates philosophy from theology, but that it *denies the possibility of theology as a science;* just as the work of Kant will consist in *denying the possibility of metaphysics as a science.* It is the progressive lopping-off of the summits of human intellectuality, the debasement of our speculative understanding, which accompanies, according to the only too true remark of Blanc de Saint-

Bonet, the progressive "weakening of Reason" in modern times.

Descartes himself did not systematically contemplate these remote consequences of his philosophical reform as far as theology was concerned. His ambition was to supplant Aristotle in philosophy. As a result, Scholastic theology, which had assumed the philosophy of Aristotle, was for him the principal and most dangerous obstance. This theology he guarded against by means of the most skilful and expert tactics; against it he nourished a secret hatred and scorn the virulence of which we can sense by certain things he let slip: "It is by their Scholastic theology," he said to young Burman, "that the monks have given rise to all the sects and heresies—by that Scholastic theology which, above all, must be swept away, *ante omnia exterminanda.* And what need is there for so much bother, since we see the illiterates and the peasants, *idiotas ac rusticos,* as well able to get to heaven as we are? That should be a warning to us that it is infinitely preferable to have a theology as simple as they, rather than to twist it by a flock of controversies, and thus corrupt it, and give occasion for disputes, quarrels, wars and other calamities. And all the more so because the theologians of one party have so got into the habit of overwhelming those in the opposing party with all sorts of calumny to the extent that they have become past masters in the art of slander, and could scarcely do otherwise than calumniate, even inadvertently."[106] Descartes expresses the same sentiments, although in less violent form, in the letter-preface to the French translation of the *Principles:* the "controversies of the School," "rendering those who study them imperceptibly more captious and self-opinionated, are perhaps the primary cause of the heresies and dissensions which now torment the world." Whereas "my principles," certainly only "very clear and very certain" truths, "will remove all subjects of dispute, and thus incline minds to gentleness and concord."[107] Scholastic theology has sown discord, Science will make us like lambs . . .

No doubt Descartes' hostility seems to bear not only on the theologian disciples of Aristotle but also on all theologians in general, nay even on theology itself, and it was indeed difficult to prevent such a natural shifting from taking place. But still, what he had directly and precisely in view was Scholastic theology,[108] in so far as it was Scholastic, not as theology. And he doubtless thought that Aristotle being an impostor, and he himself the founder of the "true Philosophy," the theology of the future—whose role would in any case be reduced, as we have seen,[109] to the purely negative and extrinsic defense of revealed truth—the theology of the future would only have to make use of Cartesian principles instead of using those of Aristotle: which could evidently not be accomplished without bringing about profound changes in theology itself. But this was not Descartes' concern, it was the business only of the theologians who were to work upon his foundation (and there were plenty of them, even too many, in the second half of the seventeenth century . . .) Did not Descartes himself boast of "showing that there was no opinion in their philosophy (the Aristotelians') which fitted in with faith, as well as his own"?[110] And despite his carefulness, in spite of his resolution not to apply reason to things of faith did he not, in his haste to assure the success of his Physics, take too many risks in strange incursions into the theology of the Eucharist, which he claimed to have completely transformed by his theory of extension-substance? Incursions unfortunate in more than one sense, for they brought about the condemnation of Cartesianism by the Index and by the Inquisition.

Thus, in Descartes himself developed a struggle, silent but merciless, not against theology as such, but against Scholastic theology (and certain theologians, Father Gibieuf in particular, seem in the first place to have encouraged him in this direction); with a new philosophy, a new theology will follow. The result seems to show clearly enough that one cannot grapple with Scholastic theology without grappling with theology itself; or break with St. Thomas without breaking with sacred wisdom . . .

Descartes' error here was to belittle and to misunderstand the nature of theology among the sciences, as it was to belittle and misunderstand the role of the Church in the intellectual government of humanity.

It is true enough that, as theology is able in fact to exist *in us* only by making use of human wisdom, a theological system which makes use of a mistaken philosophy will itself be mistaken; but Descartes did not see that theology, being a science *in itself* superior to and independent of our systems of human wisdom, must judge according to its light and choose for its service the philosophic system which in its hands will be the best instrument of truth, and which for that reason will itself be true. Nor did he see that the Church, not being a simple human administration of the spiritual, nor merely the archivist of the Lord, but being rather His Bride attended by His Spirit, has not as its rôle the sole function of preserving the deposit of revealed truth but rather to make the light of this truth shine forth in human intelligence. It is therefore scarcely credible that she should have had to wait for the philosophy of Descartes in order to be able to set up the true theology; hardly credible either that Scholastic theology, the theology the Church affirms as being fully her own, where her whole tradition reaches its highest point, should be an erroneous theology. (For in Descartes' time the Church had already taken St. Thomas for her *doctor communis*.) Nay more, in virtue of her essential mission constituted guardian of the natural order and of the health of reason, as well as of the supernatural order and truth, the philosophic tradition itself which she had assumed could not without temerity be held as null and void.

These considerations which I frankly acknowledge are elementary and have to do with simple common sense, but which are none the less valid on that account, enable us better to understand how the success of the Cartesian reform, if "Christian" in appearance, nay in intention as well, should logically bring about the subversion of the intellectual Christian edifice. Logically! Not, perhaps, through a rectilinear development of abstract logic, for the material causality in play in history submits the human evolution of spiritual principles to all sorts of stases, circuits and accidental arrangements; but logically, the way it is in the concrete logic of things where loose materials lead to rupture and collapse, and the avalanche unloosened above by the slightest shock, ravages the country below. Mgr. d'Hulst has described in a witty and penetrating passage the stupefaction of Descartes whom he imagines suddenly brought face to face with his philosophical progeniture. And certainly, Descartes would have been very astonished to see his descendants affirm the absolute independence of human reason with regard to revealing God; and nevertheless they are in fact his descendants, the children of his mind, the cheap Cartesians.

*
*   *

But let us leave these remote consequences of the despiritual-ization, so to speak, that the idea of theology and the relations of theology with philosophy suffered in Cartesian thought. And let us come back to the operation performed by Descartes with full consciousness: philosophy is no longer ordered to theology as to a superior science; henceforth the philosopher's work is completely self-contained, human wisdom perfects itself by its own efforts without feeling the need for a superior wisdom. Here we have the Cartesian rupture at its point of origin. Descartes "has opened up the line of thinkers who will be philosophers only."[111]

The result was a sort of derangement or "distraction" of the philosophical truths, and finally, in spite of so many geniuses, the diminution of philosophical intellectuality.

Why?

St. Thomas loves to repeat that in every order of things the lower is strengthened by its union with the higher; that is why in the kind of "continuity"[112] formed by the hierarchized degrees of pure spirits, illuminating one another, *per intuitum intellectus,* the lower angel illumined by the higher angel is strengthened within by him in his own intellectual light. Men cannot be illuminated in that manner, because they are all of the same specific degree. But something similar is found in us, in so far as a sort of spiritual union between specifically different habitus maintains an inferior habitus or virtue in contact with a superior

86

habitus or virtue. Thus the faith habitus strengthens the philosophical habitus in its own proper philosophical order with regard to a certain truth demonstrable by reason alone, such for example as the existence of God—object of science not of faith, for the philosopher—and makes it bring forth with more force, more perfection and more certitude its purely rational act of adhesion to that truth.[113] So it is that the light of theology strengthens the light of philosophy.

Let us not forget that metaphysics is a difficult thing for our minds and that the gods are jealous of our joy in it. There is only one way to stabilize it within us, and that is to order it to sacred science, which, in making use of it, elevates it. Orientated then toward those summits of supernatural truth accessible to theology alone, metaphysics reaches with more strength and more security toward the heights of the natural truth where it has its domain. If not, it will tend to descend.

Aristotle could philosophize without ordering metaphysics to a higher science (though he really had the idea of a higher contemplation, which he placed at the peak of metaphysics, and where man participates in the life of the gods), he could do so because in the first place he was living under the régime of the Gentiles, outside of the Mosaic revelation, before the Christian revelation; and because he found himself in absolutely unique conditions, exactly at the culminating point of Greek civilization and intellectuality, and because he profited by that Grecian success which could never again be found with the help of nature alone. Descartes could not philosophize in that way because he was living under the régime of the Gospel, and because Christian riches are heavy, much heavier to carry than the light crowns of pagans. By a merciless and blesséd necessity, which springs from the depths of our natural weakness and of the demands of divine love, the Christian cannot neglect the comfortings from above and the order they demand, without collapsing everywhere.

A strange and thrilling conflict this, between Descartes and Aristotle! Descartes is a sincere Christian, and a true philosopher, and, encouraged by the Reverend Cardinal de Bérulle, he wishes to give us a Christian philosophy of such a kind, as Malebranche is soon to say, that we shall not be obliged to go to pagans like Plato and Aristotle[114] to seek philosophical truth.

But is being a true philosopher and a sincere Christian enough to build up a Christian philosophy? Or does that rather call both for achievements which result from superior wisdom and light, and for foundations which, depending in themselves upon natural reason alone, are not necessarily guaranteed by the sincerity of the philosopher's faith, and can be more insecure in him than in a pagan, in spite of the most brilliant apologetic? Could it not be that this miscreant of an Aristotle, so bitterly envied by Descartes—that this Greek, much more of a realist and much less an idealist than certain Christians, may alone have succeeded —not certainly in building up a Christian philosophy— but in giving birth to the principles of reason which the Angel of the School will come to use, carrying them to a much higher degree of purity, in order to give to Christian philosophy its real and proper form? Could that not be, perhaps, because Aristotle followed most faithfully the line of nature, and doubtless also because it pleased God, in order better to establish the universality of His domain as well as the fairness of His conduct, to prepare in pagan ground, cut off from the influence of revealed faith, the work of natural reason which was to become the preferred instrument of the sacred doctrine? Winged spirits, you philosophers who believe in *the difficulties of Thomism,* and who think there is "something rotten in the principles of Aristotle," of what joys, alas, do you not deprive yourselves in your aversion to "Greek intellectualism"! By a deplorable fate, you, victims and torturers of your own selves, render yourselves incapable of admiring that marvelous encounter, achieved in St. Thomas, and where the hand of God appears so glowingly, that encounter of Hellenic and Aristotelian reason—whose very deficiencies and inadequacy and narrowness, sometimes tragic but redeemed by such vigor, accentuate its wholly human beauty—with the divine splendors of the revelation of the Son and of the madness of the Gospel. You render yourselves incapable of that joy which would have been pleasing to you, of seeing the principles Aristotle discovered in the obscurity of human wisdom (and which command metaphysical problems such as those of Knowledge and Intelligence, Will, of Life, Action and Generation), blossom out into theological treatises like that of the Trinity, and blossom fully only there, in the radiant night—*et nox illuminatio mea in deliciis meis*—brilliant as day, the night of revealed mysteries.

When I, a simple and ingenuous follower of Cajetan and of John of St. Thomas, succeed in tasting, thanks to these masters and in the measure of my weakness, the intelligible beauties which these sacred disputations disclose, it seems to me that I am enjoying undeservedly a good which should be common to all Christians, and to you particularly, philosophers and scholars, whose souls are a cup of great price made to hold the delicious wine of truth.

But I apologize for giving way, if only for an instant, to sentiments which run the risk of appearing romantic, and moreover,

according to the common fate of sentiments, of being misunderstood by those very people who have given rise to them . . .
As I was saying, Aristotle could have been taken over by Christian
wisdom, precisely because he succeeded, through a unique bit of
luck and in spite of the errors of which he certainly was not
free, in establishing the essential principles of metaphysics according to the demands of pure natural reason, and because Thomas
Aquinas transfigured, strengthened and deepened that metaphysics
in ordering it to the superior truth of theology. As for Descartes,
eager to invent a more Christian and more spiritualistic philosophy, more simple and more angelic than that of St. Thomas, he
allows preoccupations which come to him through his faith and
even elements which derive from theology to filter into his
philosophy itself, at the expense of its solidity. But that simplified
and fragile philosophy he orders only to itself; philosophy is
no longer to be strengthened and illumined by theology. And
thus he shatters the foremost and highest of the hierarchical
subordinations, the essential order which wills that in the vital
economy of Christian intelligence, metaphysics, while keeping
its autonomy as queen of human sciences, and depending intrinsically on rational evidence alone, should be placed under the
superior light of theological wisdom and of supernatural truth.

DESCARTES AND METAPHYSICS

In the moral realm one cannot throw off the supernatural
order without warping at the same time the order of nature, for
nature itself requires that order should be everywhere acknowledged. In the realm of wisdom it is the same, and Descartes'
offense against the theoelogical order necessarily is accompanied

by an offense against the philosophical order. Turning aside from the mysterious lights which used to dominate it, philosophy which had once been Christian undergoes an upsetting of its internal order, the hierarchy proper to philosophy is subverted.

This subversion asserts itself so clearly, so bluntly in Descartes, that it is not necessary in this case to go into as many details as were dealt with on the subject of theology. We know that "the principal rule . . . observed" by him "in his studies" was that he "never used more than very few hours a day in thoughts which occupy the imagination, and very few hours in the year in those which occupy understanding alone."[115] "Just as I believe," he added, "that it is very necessary to have understood clearly, once in one's lifetime, the principles of metaphysics, because they give us the knowledge of God and of our soul, so I believe it would be very harmful to occupy one's understanding in frequent meditation of them, because it could not then so easily busy itself with the functions of the imagination and the senses." In the *Discourse on Method* he contrasts the new philosophy with the old in that the old was speculative, and the new is to be "practical," and will make us "masters and possessors of nature." In the *Principles* he represents philosophy or science as a tree whose roots are Metaphysics, whose trunk is Physics, and whose branches are Medicine, Mechanics and Ethics; Metaphysics does nothing then but fasten the tree of science to the soil and begin the production of the sap. The fruit—the delectable ultimate, according to the ancients—we are to demand of the practical sciences.

The Cartesian upsetting[116] consists then in making metaphysics the first part and no longer the last, the beginning and not the end, the base and no longer the peak of philosophy—a useful organ and no longer the head; an upsetting of capital importance one might say, since it amounts to putting the head in the place of the feet, or even—if Aristotle is right in comparing a plant to a living animal whose mouth would be buried in the soil—precisely to transforming into a plant, into a tree, that Philosophy to which the gods have given as to a reasoning animal, a visage raised toward heaven, *os sublime* . . .

It is often said that Descartes is first of all a physicist and a scientist: that is true as far as his predilections are concerned, true also with regard to his most genuine claims to glory and to his most inspired activity. But Descartes is not a "positivist" scientist such as we see about us nowadays; he remains substantially a metaphysician—and that is why he has done so much harm to metaphysics, which can be hurt only by its own. Descartes is a metaphysician unfaithful to metaphysics, who turns aside voluntarily toward the plains, toward the vast, flat country watered by the river Mathematics; a metaphysician who does not like metaphysical truth, who finds this too-white manna tasteless, and who makes his way, followed by countless people, toward the savory onions of the physical world.

In claiming to base everything on metaphysics Descartes in reality prepares the ruin of metaphysics: as a matter of fact he twists and vitiates its bearing from the beginning, starting off immediately by the pure intelligible instead of reaching it progressively beginning with sense data: all of which is suitable for angels but not for men; it removes all scientific consistency from metaphysics, and is soon to separate it from the experimental sciences and throw it into vain pretensions to a pure *a priori;* until the moment when Kant will refuse it the right to exist as a science. From another point of view Descartes appears to us as having, properly speaking, *degraded* metaphysics, in the sense that neglecting the specific superiority and, if I may say so, the sublimity of its degree of abstraction, he requires of it expeditious procedure, a facility, a manageability only suitable to the less noble degree of intelligibility of mathematics; he weakens it therefore in proportion as he takes away its means and its very weapons, and imposes upon it the law of an inferior discipline.

Finally and above all the fact of ordering metaphysics to positive science has, with regard to metaphysics itself, significance and consequences which it is essential to stress. If Descartes goes in for metaphysics, it is *for the sake of* physics; if he is interested in divine perfections, it is in order to deduce from them the first laws of matter, to descend from God to things; he is only interested in metaphysics to the extent that, assuring the legitimacy of human science and the bases of physics, it justifies, nay more, it really lays the foundations, in his eyes, of the knowledge of this world and the detail of its phenomena; he plunges "for once in his life" straight into the intelligible, but only to remain there the shortest possible time, and to go as soon as possible into the less austere regions where the understanding holds sway with the imagination and the senses. In other words, if we might hark back to the great Augustinian distinction between the *uti* and the *frui,* the sovereign speculation of the most lofty truths accessible to reason ceases to be an end and a pure object of *fruition,* it will henceforth be a means, indispensible perhaps, but a means which must be used for the knowledge of the sensible world and its phenomena—and in the last analysis, in the interests of practice; there in Descartes is the very first root of the pragmatism and the utilitarianism which so curiously characterize the modern conception of science.

The process finally amounts to depriving metaphysics of its normal conditions of existence and of handing it over to the arbitrary. This preëminently free science, whose nobility consists in being of all human disciplines the most completely self-contained, *maxime propter seipsam,* this *dea scientiarum* is thus condemned to withdraw into darkness; for its gaze becomes clouded if the preoccupation of worldly attainments and human purposes sweeps down upon the leisure of such a scandalously speculative wisdom, wholly absorbed in observing—a wisdom completely detached from the secondary preoccupation of applications (wherein it differs from the special sciences); and which on the other hand, unlike the higher wisdom which comes from the Holy Spirit, is not a wisdom of life as it is one of truth. If in order to remain fixed in intelligible being it does not subject and order the whole matter of experience to itself, it loses its vigor and its equilibrium; in the spiritual world of virtues and *habitus* much more surely than in our human world, the superior cannot live if it is under obedience to the inferior.

"Spinoza Begins . . ."

In virtue of the metaphysical primacy of the intelligence among our faculties, the order of the intelligence is primordial among all human orders. To interfere with that order, to shift the intellectual hierarchies about, is to meddle with the primary and most vital of the mysterious dominants of any order of ours. It is not that the consequences of such a fault are immediately manifest, nor that the material of it presents much bulk: it is a fault completely imperceptible to the senses and, as it were, angelic; it is none the less serious, the invisible crumbling is not the least tragic.

If with the ancients we consider science, in so far as it is distinguished from wisdom, as the knowledge of secondary causes and of all the created detail in contrast to the knowledge of primary causes and of the uncreated Principle, we should say that the capital error of Descartes is to have suppressed theoretically this distinction between science and wisdom (which become identified for him in *Philosophy,* which is above all practical),* and to have, in fact, ordered wisdom to science, and therefore to have preferred science to wisdom. A preference which is the great sin of the modern world, and appears as a similitude and a springing forth again, in proportion to our pettiness, of an older sin by which we also hoped to become like unto the gods.

It has been said: *the Truth shall make you free.* But which truth, that of mathematics or that of faith can, absolutely speaking, make man free? Neither metaphysical nor theological wisdom, but only the wisdom of the saints can, in making us "gods by participation," given us perfect freedom. For Descartes, it is by science, especially by mathematics, that man becomes autonomous,** and that in submitting the forces of material nature to the reign of his artifices and his technique he will gain his freedom.

---

* Descartes knows very well that wisdom is the highest perfection of the intellect, but he calls wisdom "that perfect knowledge of everything that man can know," which is specifically one, of the very unity of the understanding, and which, beginning with metaphysics and constituting itself through physics, finds its fulfilment in mechanics, medicine and ethics.

** See note 65.

THE DREAM OF DESCARTES

In so far as he has in fact introduced the principle of the isolation and of the sufficiency of human science (and from this principle were to follow the separation of philosophy from theology and even the elimination of theology altogether as a science), and furthermore, in so far as he has reduced metaphysics to sustain physics, the science of phenomena, and human experience, and has thus prepared the final ruin of metaphysics, it must be said that Descartes, doubtless unintentionally, but nevertheless effectively, is at the origin of the great movement by which reason is to break with the God of revealed faith and to abandon little by little the God of Metaphysics—in short, to withdraw from Him Who is.

Finally, just what is it to prefer science to wisdom, and to orientate all learning toward the conquest of the created, if not to tend toward naturalism? There is thus, still enclosed in its causes and not brought out, a whole naturalism latent in Descartes: naturalism of reason, the formula for which Spinoza will soon provide and which must inevitably—some hundred years later—give way to the naturalism of the instinct and the sentiment, the welling-up of the old spirit of the Lutheran revolution modernized and rendered effeminate by Jean-Jacques. The expression of Leibnitz: "Spinoza begins where Descartes leaves off, by naturalism,"[117] takes its full force here, like the remark Bossuet made when he was finally disillusioned about the new philosophy he had too long harbored: "I see . . . a great combat being prepared against the Church, in the name of Cartesian philosophy."[118]

We find several indications of this naturalism latent in

Descartes in the very doctrine of the philosopher. Do not the theologians teach us[119] that in the state of nature fallen and redeemed, if indeed reason remains "physically" capable of knowing with its strength alone every truth of the natural order, it is still not *morally possible* that without the help of revelation it should succeed in discovering and bringing together in their purity all these speculative and practical truths? Now Descartes is profoundly convinced that we are perfectly able to arrive by reason alone—cut off from faith—at *"a perfect knowledge of all philosophy"* as *"the highest degree of wisdom,"*[120] and at *"a perfect knowledge of everything that man can know,* as much for the conduct of his life as for the conservation of his health and the invention of all the arts."[121] A dogmatic presumption which involves a radical negation of the notion of Christian philosophy, which a humbler and truer idea of our nature would have spared the new philosophy.

Descartes is equally convinced of the moral possibility that we possess of arriving by reason alone at a practical wisdom and a "perfection of life" complete in the order of natural virtues— to which can be added afterwards the superstructure of Christian virtues—as if in the present state of human nature we could acquire without the help of grace, full perfection in the realm of natural morality. Does he not call the ethics which issues from the tree of philosophy—thus from reason alone—*"the highest and most perfect Ethics,* which, presupposing a complete knowledge of other sciences, is the last degree of Wisdom"?[122] These few words are capable of wide repercussions, and they enable us to realize that the philosopher, if he was meditating especially on ethics, had always been careful to write very little on the subject, out of prudence.[123] In saying that the highest and most perfect Ethics *presupposes a complete knowledge of the other sciences* he practically tells us that until his reform this highest and most perfect Ethics was not known—since until his reform no philosopher had arrived at "certain knowledge of anything"[124] in the sciences. He also tells us that it is science which will give us this ethics; this latter, being able to reach its full perfection only by presupposing the perfect knowledge of physics and of medicine, depends upon the scientific conquest of the material world by man, which throws us right into the middle of the "scientist" and naturalist illusion. On the one hand, therefore, he makes the sole end of human life here below be the "full realization of reason,"[125] and he is persuaded that we shall manage *through science* to subject nature *completely,* within us and outside of us, to our reason which will then become effectively the queen of nature.[126] On the other hand, reason for him, tends completely to regulate human acts, and this not as a secondary cause acting *in virtute primae causae* (as a participation or a created derivation—forever indigent and imperfect in some respect—of the eternal Law, *summa ratio in Deo existens*)[127] but by virtue of supreme authority guaranteed extrinsically and once and for all by divine veracity. It is considerations such as there, in fact, which cause theologians like Bishop Chollet[128] and Father Lucien Roure to agree with Mr. Liard[130] in seeing in Descartes a distant ancestor of godless ethics.

Let us not forget that upon occasion the philosopher admits in the present state of our nature the existence of a natural love of God which makes Him loved efficaciously above everything else: "I have no doubt," he wrote to Chanut in a letter intended for Queen Christine, "that we can really love God by the sole strength of our nature. I do not guarantee that this love is meritorious without grace, I leave that for the theologians to settle; but I make bold to say that in regard to this life it is the most ravishing and most useful passion that we can have, and even that it can be *the strongest passion,* although for that one might certainly need a concentrated meditation, because we are continually diverted by the presence of other objects. Now the path which I judge one should follow to arrive at the love of God is that one must bear in mind that He is a spirit or thing which thinks . . . If with that one notices the infinity of His power . . . the extent of His providence . . . the infallibility of His decrees . . . and finally, our pettiness on the one hand—on the other, the grandeur of all created things . . .[131] the meditation of all these things fills a man who understands them with a joy so extreme . . . that of his own accord completely uniting with Him *he loves Him so perfectly that he desires nothing else in the world,* save that God's will be done."[132] The tone of that whole letter is magnificent. Let us be careful to note, however, that Descartes here again transposes Christianity on to the plane of reason alone, and that this love of God, so perfect, is not due to grace-given charity; it is due only to "the strength of our nature alone" and of philosophical mediation: we are nearer than it might appear to the *amor intellectualis Dei* of Spinoza.

Let us recall that for Descartes the aim of knowledge is effectively to procure for us here below, along with the mastery of the world and of our passions, and along with a marvelously increased longevity, a natural beatitude, "sovereign good of human life" [134]—to which the Christian adds besides the well-founded hope of heavenly beatitude. We conclude that the naturalism of Descartes if it had been explicit, would no doubt have found its expression in a theological formula such as the following: original sin has not left any *wounds* in our nature; man is born today in a state in no way less good than the state of pure nature, itself conceived as very good; or more precisely: we live under the régime of pure nature, which the régime of grace is only entrusted to crown; in the state of fact in which human nature finds itself, reason suffices by its natural forces alone to make humanity live reasonably, and to procure the good of men and of peoples. Descartes, certain of whose metaphysical theories were to be exploited by the Jansenists, takes up his position here at the extreme opposite of Jansenism, and one sees a Pelagian optimism appear in him, limited to the rational and spiritual parts of the human being, an optimism of Reason, fore-runner of the sentimental optimism of the eighteenth century, and which is even like a very distant, hardly perceptible prelude to the irrational optimism which Jean-Jacques Rousseau was to promulgate on an entirely different plane and with a far greater amplitude.

In order to measure the importance of this evolution of the intellect in the direction of naturalism since the Cartesian reform, one has only to think of the astonishing change under-gone in a few centuries by the meaning of the word science. For the Christian doctors, the science *par excellence* was the science which is at the same time wisdom—*sapientia per modum cognitionis,* that is to say metaphysics, the supreme fruit of purely human speculation, and far above it, theology, which is a kind of impression within us[185] of the holy science that God has of Himself—and higher even than that, science no longer of the discursive mode, but of the mystic mode, *sapientia per modum inclinationis,* the wisdom of the saints. For Descartes science is all human learning taken in its unity, and fructifying in Medicine, Mechanics, and Ethics. For the moderns, science, speaking absolutely, is the putting of observable phenomena into mathematical or tangible formulas, "positive" science, which is akin to opinion as well as to knowledge, which teaches us nothing about the substance and causes of the physical world considered in their very being, and whose task it is simply to spread over the physical world, for the purpose of subjecting it to our practical needs, to our industry, to our desire for well-being, an immense network of quantitative relations and of theories which save sensible appearances. Although we put it to a use of perdition, this science is good in itself; but what is extraordinary, and what gives some idea of the lowering of intellectual values during the last two centuries, is the fact that it had reabsorbed into itself the whole meaning of the great and terrible word Science.

Some years after the philosopher's death faith in the *true and useful Philosophy* became universal. Huygens was convinced that the Academy of Sciences would arrive at "the knowledge of the causes of nature" in working "at natural history somewhat after the outline of Verulam." "To know what gravity is," he cried, "what is heat, cold, the attraction of the magnet, light, colors; what elements go to make up air, water, fire and all the other bodies; the purpose of respiration in animals; how metals, stones and plants develop; of all these things little or nothing is yet known, *there being nevertheless nothing in the world* the knowledge of which would be more desirable or more useful . . ." The usefulness of these experiments will extend "to the whole of mankind, and for all time to come." And Oldenbourg writes to Huygens in 1666: "I hope that in time all nations, with the slightest claims to being civilized, will embrace one another as cherished companions, and will pool all their strength, of the mind as well as of material wealth, in order to banish ignorance and make supreme the true and useful philosophy."

It should be remarked here that what gave strength and momentum to Descartes, while it assumed in him a rational form, was that powerful movement of the human heart toward the possession of the tangible world and its mysteries, and toward the domination, taken as ultimate end in itself, of nature and the corporeal universe, which characterized the scientific enthusiasm of the Renaissance, and which before finding with Galileo and especially with Descartes a purely rational instrument in the physico-mathematical method, had sometimes had recourse to strange collusions with magic and occultism. An attack of spiritual concupiscence which shows us that whereas the intellectual order in a Christian world wishes to complete metaphysical and theological wisdom with the wisdom of the Holy Spirit, which stabilizes all the hierarchies of the intellect in the very heart of God, by connaturalizing man to his supreme object—similarly, by virtue of the same law the first tremor of this intellectual order could not have been due to reason alone, but first of all to a breath of desire, to a certain love, to a diversion of the whole soul, which has the appearance, in short, of a mystical covetousness of the earth.

Nevertheless, it rested with the intellect itself to make the break effective and expressly to begin the destruction of the intellectual order. That was the work of Cartesian reason. But all this takes place in the heights of the mind, in a region where it is easy to understand that our gaze could not penetrate if we were not willing to proceed as metaphysicians, and if we were to dwell on the materiality of doctrines, without paying attention to their formal principles.

CHAPTER IV

THE CARTESIAN PROOFS OF GOD

THE CARTESIAN PROOFS OF GOD

PORTRAIT OF THE INFINITE

It is not my intention in this chapter to comment in all their detail upon the three Cartesian proofs of the existence of God: that is, by the existence of the idea of the Infinite within us; by our own existence in so far as we imagine the Infinite; or by the very essence of the Perfect which we think. Assuming that the reader has these in mind, I shall try only to emphasize their essential logical line, as in a diagram, in order to bring out their presuppositions, and to make their value clearer.

The first Cartesian proof, unlike the third, has had no historical influence. Nevertheless, the philosopher attributed a major importance to that construction, which he so carefully and minutely studied. It seemed to him conclusive. Hence our special interest in this proof. It has to do with a certain conception of ideas, a strictly and specifically Cartesian conception, through which, in fact, but only through which, it has compelling force. It is, so to speak, the rational display and putting into effect of this conception of ideas, and at the same time it gives us the best confirmation of the importance it had in Descartes' mind: I refer to the theory of *idea-pictures*.

I have already had several occasions to speak of these idea-pictures.[186] Mr. Désiré Roustan asked me one day if I attributed

107

that expression to Descartes himself. I have never stated that he used it, and it was not in the least necessary for him to do so. It is enough that it exactly characterizes his thought. In any case, we get the word directly from Descartes: "My natural intelligence enables me to know evidently that my ideas are in me like pictures . . ."[187]

Whatever the facts may be regarding the word itself, it is quite certain that in keeping, it would seem, with the current seventeenth century usage of the language, but extracting from that usage a metaphysical value unnoticed by others, Descartes looked upon ideas as images or pictures painted in the soul. These constituted the mind's immediate object within the soul. Whether they be of the tangible order or of the intelligible order, these ideas, which have now become objects or things, cause us to know, immediately and in themselves, nothing but images traced in our thought and bearing resemblance to things. That is why our understanding is infallible when it is content to contemplate them without affirming or denying anything.

Descartes thus transposed into his system a classic thesis of ancient philosophy, according to which the intellect "is never mistaken" in the simple apprehension of the objects of thought. But the difference in meaning between the Scholastic thesis and the Cartesian thesis was fundamental. In the latter, these objects primarily apprehended are the ideas themselves (terms *quod*, images of a thing); in the former they were the "natures" or possible realities (*quidditates*) apprehended by and in the concepts (terms *quo*), without these concepts themselves being known as objects, unless through an ulterior reflection. From this follows an equally fundamental difference which has to do with the theory of judgment. For the Scholastics, if truth or falsehood is the attribute of judgment, or of the "second operation of the mind," it is because at this point the mind unites its objects of concept—the intelligible natures mentioned above— and because this composition may or may not correspond to the behavior of *what is* (in actual or possible existence). For Descartes on the contrary, it is because at this point the mind, by a voluntary movement or consent, takes the idea-object or idea-picture which it perceives within itself, as being conformable to an actual or possible extramental counterpart, and because this conformity may or may not be real in fact.

There are numerous texts in which Descartes shows that for him ideas are idea-pictures.[138] The controversy between Arnauld and Malebranche,[139] for instance, brought out in a particularly suggestive way, both the importance the Cartesian school attached to this conception of the "representative ideas," and the inability of our classical era to rediscover the true notion of the concept, in opposition to Descartes.

"I have often served notice that I take the word 'idea' to indicate anything immediately conceived by the mind . . . and I have used this word because it had already been generally accepted by philosophers to mean the forms of the conceptions of divine understanding, although we do not recognize in God any fantasy or corporeal imagination; and I could think of no more appropriate term."[140] This answer to an objection by Hobbes attests an historic filiation which we were already justified in assuming because of the theoretically discernable relationship between the Cartesian "idea" and the "creative idea" in the sense the ancients gave it.

The Scholastics preferred to call 'idea' the idea not of the knowing agent but of the artist, the preconceived form, the intellectual matrix of a work to be created. The characteristic of such an idea is that it does not present to the mind an object which is a thing independent of the mind, and to which it happens to be known; this idea presents to the mind the pattern of a thing to be made, an object which consequently precedes that thing, and to which that thing will conform.

God Himself thinking Himself sees in His essence all its possible participations or imitations; the divine essence seen in this light, as a transcendent and infinite exemplar in whose resemblance all things are creatable and created and known—known before existing in their own nature and as always present in creative eternity—that is what constituted for the Scholastics the divine ideas,[141] and which Descartes will call "the forms of the conceptions of divine understanding, *formas perceptionum mentis divinae.*"

Let us suppose then that by a double process of veering toward materiality (for which the primary responsibility doubtless goes back to the Scholastic routine) the ideas of the human artist are regarded in the first place not as a pure spiritual intuition, simple and transcendent with regard to the work (*res ideata*) to be formed by it, but as an ideal counterpart of the thing, a ready-made model which the artist contemplates in his mind and which he has only to copy in order to realize it outside of his mind. Then in the second place let us suppose that the philosopher, yielding inadvertently to our anthropomorphic imagination, conceives the divine ideas themselves as being a multitude of models or of duplicates to be traced off, which God presumably contemplates in His thought, and after the fashion of which He creates things.

THE CARTESIAN PROOFS OF GOD

Let us next suppose that an initial confusion or transposition brings it about that what pertains to human *knowing* is conceived according to the type of divine *art,* itself conceived in the manner just explained. The relation between these divine models and the things created which are copies of them, or, more generally speaking, between the operative idea of the artist (understood as explained above) and the copy which is executed from it, finds itself transferred from the order of *making* to the order of *knowing,* and is applied to the relation between the concept and the thing known. The role of model or examplar will then pass from the (creative) idea to the thing (known), and the role of the copy or the image will pass from the thing (made) to the (cognitive) idea. There will be a criss-crossing of the terms, and for the relation of idea-pattern to ideate-copy will be substituted the relation of idea-portrait to ideate-model.

We shall then have the Cartesian notion of ideas,[142] which comes straight from the notion of the "forms of the conceptions of the divine understanding." Once the philosopher has established the existence of God, he will hold these ideas to be innate and in conformity with their models or "patterns," and this he will do in the name of the veracity of the God who created both. Before he has established the existence of God, and beginning with the *cogito,* he knows (this is the Cartesian postulate) that they are objects immediately apprehended by his thought within itself, but he does not yet know, or at least has not guarded against a possible doubt, whether these objects are, or are not— as he is inclined to believe by an impulse which might conceivably come from a mischievous genius as well as from the natural light of the intelligence—the authentic portraits of things which exist or can exist outside himself.

111

Since our ideas present to us as objects primarily attained only themselves, it is of supreme importance to distinguish what should and what should not be attributed to the natural light of the understanding in the impulse just mentioned. Is it that light which leads us to believe that clear and distinct ideas are true pictures presenting to the mind, at the same time as they present themselves, a thing or "nature" of which they are the image? Yes, indeed, but we shall know it for certain only after an ample metaphysical research, and thanks in particular to the whole process of the *cogito* and of the proofs of the existence of God. And this is not the case with confused ideas, particularly ideas of sensible qualities and affections. Examination will show that the impulse which leads us to regard these ideas as true portraits making known other things than themselves, is a blind and a rash one; for after all, if matter exists, as the philosopher will laboriously prove in his last *Meditation*, there is nevertheless no resemblance between what it is, which is something completely geometric, and the picture which those ideas offer us.[148] Thus are mutually strengthened "my physics" which is completely mechanicist and "my metaphysics" which is wholly angelical. Turn thou away from the senses, O my soul, in so far as they claim to acquaint thee with the corporeal realities and with the delusive world here below (which in truth is not deceptive at all; it is the senses which deceive us, but in the infinity of the extension governed by the laws of movement, the understanding finds perfect rest). It is through God, after thyself and within thyself, that thou must begin to know; through God, Whose existence, if it were possible, thou shouldst grasp (but the weight of discourse prevents thee) in the same intuition in which thou graspest thine own existence and thine own thought. As Malebranche put it later, it is enough to think of God to have Him exist.*

It is clear—but it is a stroke of genius to have been the first to see it so strongly—that if our ideas are our only immediate objects, the whole existence of things becomes doubtful. The problem of existence, then, takes the foremost place in Descartes' preoccupations.

But a still more serious problem exists in the background. It is the problem of the possible, or of the value of our ideas in relation to the essences themselves. We have immediate assurance of our ideas alone; what is to guarantee to us that they represent real essences, true possibles, and that in the intelligible order itself they are not "materially false"?

After enunciating the maxim that the intellect in simple apprehension is never mistaken, the Scholastics immediately corrected or defined it more accurately. They went on to explain that the intellect can still be mistaken by accident, in so far as in the very perception of the intelligibles itself a composition of notions[144] can intervene (hence an implicit judgment of compatibility); it is then possible that an *ens rationis*, an entity of pure imagination—for example, a complex made up of incompossible notes—may be presented to the mind as if it were an essence. What we have in such cases is an object of thought, or a pseudo-object of thought, that the mind conceives *ad instar entis* and which is not a possible reality. The same restriction imposes itself upon Descartes, although in him it takes on a different meaning. Because for him it is not a question of an object which is seized in an idea and is not a possible reality, but of an idea itself which is seized upon as object and is not the portrait of any

---

* If then one thinks of Him, He must exist." (*Recherches de la Vérité,* bk. IV, ch. xi.)

possible model.[145]   And the philosopher knows that this is precisely the case with a great number of ideas, with those ideas of the senses such as the idea of cold and of heat which we rashly accept under the impression we are following the natural light; ideas which led ancient physics astray.

The fact that there are entities of pure imagination did not occasion any especially tragic questioning for Aristotle's metaphysics, because in the first place Aristotle knew that the first intuition of the intelligence, bearing upon being, bears evidently upon a possible reality, and not upon an *ens rationis,* and that furthermore no construction intervenes in it; and because, in the second place, acknowledging the value of sense experience—the source of all our ideas—and having through this experience an existing reality, he was sure *a fortiori* that what he had was in fact a possible reality. For Descartes on the contrary, the fact that there are ideas which are materially false raised a terribly disturbing question; for he starts from his thought alone and from what he reads in it, and such a fact threatened from the outset to prevent any bridging over from thought to things, by a preliminary obstacle which concerned the very possibility of those things even before their existence.

Descartes, indeed, cannot suppose that a clear and distinct idea is not true, as long as he ponders over it, because it thrusts itself then and there, evident and resistant, upon his understanding, as though free from any hidden incompossibility. But let him once turn aside from it, and behold: withdrawn from the constraining influx of clarity, he will begin to wonder whether the idea *was not* a misleading one. The hypothesis of the deceiving God or of the mischievous Genius gives body to this doubt— a doubt that is "hyperbolical" and "metaphysical" because in this case it militates against the natural light itself. But for that very same reason, it is a fundamentally important doubt, one which affects the very essence of thought. Does this mean that we are at the centre of a conflict of the natural light of reason with itself, of evidence with evidence? The sole idea of a deceiving God or of a mischievous Genius shows me clearly that I can be mistaken even in that which appears to me with the utmost clarity.[146]

Now, among all the ideas that I enumerate within me, I perceive one that is " the clearest and most distinct of all those in my mind," therefore "the truest."[147] Is not "everything that my mind conceives clearly and distinctly as being real and true and which contains within itself any perfection, entirely contained and enclosed in this idea?" I shall fix my eyes upon it, I shall not take my attention from it until it has delivered me from the supreme doubt. It is the idea of the Infinite. As long as I ponder it, any chance of imagining that it does not represent a possible reality disappears. What is more real than what is perfect?[148]

The whole question then is: is this idea going to enable me to pass from the possible to the existent, is it going to assure me that the possible model which it represents, exists?

Descartes here invokes (in the name of the natural light of the understanding, without going into any particular critical examination),* the principle of causality, in a very significant

---

* The criterion of clear and distinct ideas defined in a somewhat empirical way immediately following the *cogito*, seems to him a sufficient "justification" of first principles, at least in so far as they are actually thought. And this is probably so because doubt bears *above all* upon the affirmations of existence, and because on the other hand, it is in fact powerless before actually constraining evidences. Nevertheless the fact remains that Descartes has extended it even to those principles which hitherto he had regarded as self-evident (see note 146); finally, it seems to us impossible for Descartes to avoid the reproach of reasoning in a vicious circle.

form. The natural light assures him that the cause should contain within itself, formally or eminently, at least as much reality as its effect. Now what effect must here be accounted for?—My idea of God. But that idea as a modification of my thought, as an entity in me—we would say nowadays, that idea as a state of consciousness—Descartes said in the language of the School, the *formal reality* of that idea? Not at all. But rather the *objective reality* of this idea, or the object that it shows me, that is to say in the Cartesian sense, this idea itself as an object presented to the mind, as a picture seen, and all the perfection it contains in that capacity. The principle of causality then takes the following form there should be, formally or eminently, at least as much reality and perfection in the total and efficient cause of my ideas as there are objective reality and objective perfection in these ideas themselves. Suppose we say: there should be actually as much beauty in the cause of the portrait as there is beauty represented in it.

Now, great as the beauty portrayed in a picture may be, one can always suppose, as long as it is a finite beauty, that the painter and all the effective beauty of his gifts, of his imagination and of his art, suffices to explain or account for it; he might have invented this picture, which will then be a portrait without a model. One can suppose that the effective perfections which are in me suffice to account for the perfection of all my ideas in so far as they are objects or portraits: I mean for the objective perfection of all my ideas—all but the idea of the Infinite! If I find portrayed in a picture an infinite beauty, Beauty itself, no finite painter could have drawn it from himself, the picture must be the portrait of a model which itself has *caused* that beauty in imprinting its image upon the canvas, and which, as efficient cause, contains within itself, formally or eminently, at least as much beauty as there is objective or represented beauty in the picture. As Louis Racine puts it:

Quelle main, quel pinceau dans mon âme a tracé
D'un objet infini l'image incomparable?*

Thus the portrait of the Infinite which exists in me has enabled me to pass over to the existence of its Author, Who can only be the Infinite Himself. I have only to look at this idea-portrait to be certain that it portrays a possible reality: but by means of the principle of causality which I bring into play as I contemplate this idea, I see that as cause of the perfection it represents, it requires a cause at least as effectively perfect, and which will have caused it to exist in me; and precisely because an existing reality must be the cause of it, I know that it portrays an existing reality.[149] Thanks to the principle of causality I am certain that my idea of God resembles a "pattern" or an "original" which exists outside of me and of which it is the portrait.

From there on, this God being wholly perfect and veracious— no more of a deceiving God or mischievous genius! In God I rest all my knowledge. There is nothing certain for the atheist. God guarantees me the value of the natural light itself, and that all my clear and distinct ideas are true ideas, portraits of truly possible essences, and He guarantees thus by His truthfulness that the sense-ideas themselves, if they do not represent things as they are, come nevertheless, as from the cause or the occasion which excites them in me, from a corporeal matter which truly

* What hand, what brush has etched within my soul
  The incomparable image of an infinite object?

exists, and which in its essence is only mobile extension. The existence of the world is found again.

Thus Descartes in his first proof means to establish the existence of God by His effects, but his approach is fundamentally different from that of the Scholastics. The effect that he has chosen is not a reality existing in the world, it is an idea existing in his thought, the idea of the Infinite or of the Perfect. He thinks by this means to gain a great advantage over traditional philosophy. He does not need either the world or any existing reality except his own thought. He is also dispensed from any considering of the possibility or impossibility of progress to infinity in the series of causes. He passes immediately from the idea of God—that is, from the perfection represented in this idea—to God Himself as Cause of the idea. His proof however, necessarily presupposes his very particular conception of ideas. It fades away if this conception is false.

Caterus was on the right track when he answered Descartes: the "objective reality" of our ideas needs no cause.—What does this mean? The object presented by our ideas is not our ideas, it is the thing rendered, thanks to them, object of thought. One can try to find what cause thus brings things to the condition of object presented to the mind: it is the mind itself (making use of what it has received from things through the senses). But there is no perfection of the object which duplicates the perfection of the thing, and to seek the cause of the very perfection of the object presented in the idea is to seek the cause of the perfection of the thing itself, since the object is the thing and not the idea. To look for the cause of the all-perfection presented to the mind (in an imperfect mode) in the idea of God is, if God exists, to seek the cause of the all-perfection of God Himself:

or else, if God does not exist, it is to seek the cause of a merely possible object or even of an entity of pure imagination presented to the mind, that is to say of something which, having no other existence in act than to be thought, has no cause except the mind and the existing realities from which the mind drew its ideas to begin with.* Descartes chose as effect for which to seek the cause, exactly that which is not effect (neither picture nor portrait), but object (presented to the mind through an idea which itself is not, unless reflectively, object of knowledge).

Caterus however gets off the track very quickly, and rather irrelevantly applies a classical observation which deals with an entirely different question (the multiplicity of our ideas due to the weakness of the human mind). And Descartes, who regards his theory of idea-pictures as a pure evidence, cannot understand the main point of the objection made to his first proof. "If anyone has in mind the idea of some very artificial machine,"[150] "the objective artifice of that idea must have some cause, that is to say, either the science of this workman or of some other from whom he has got the idea; by the same token it is impossible that the idea of God which is within us should not have God Himself as its cause."[151] This comparison, with which the philosopher was particularly satisfied (it appears again in the *Principles*),[152] brings us back to the creative idea, object-model of an ideate-copy, on whose pattern Descartes conceives the idea as an object-copy of an ideate-model. The idea-model has as its cause the mind which constructs it (and it is quite true that

* Or in more technical language: the existence of the object of thought as such or of the known as such (*esse cognitum seu objectivum*) is purely ideal; one can seek the cause of the concept by which an object is known but not of the object (as such, as distinct *ratione* from the thing) which is known in the concept. Concerning the *esse objectivum* see below, note 196.

the idea even in so far as it is formative of a thing to be made, is only dependent upon the causality of the mind). Similarly, the idea-copy and the idea-picture will be dependent—not, like the idea as means of knowledge such as St. Thomas understood it, on the causality of the mind joined to that of things—but on a cause which is God and which imprints the idea upon us; for, once proven that this is the case for the idea of God, it is clear that it will also be the case for all our other ideas.

THE CANVAS OF THE PORTRAIT

The second Cartesian proof is merely an extension of the first. "It matters little that my second proof, based on our own existence, be considered as different from the first, or simply as an explanation of the first . . ."[153] To pass by way of causality from the idea of God over to the existence of God, one can start from this idea itself, or from the thought which contemplates this idea. Descartes has considered the portrait of the Infinite and the perfections painted there; he now considers the *subjectile* of this portrait, the canvas upon which it is drawn. What is my cause, of me, that thought which thinks God?

To start out in order to ascend right to the first cause, from my own existence—from me, a thinking subject, rather than from some other existence, is a simple variation on the theme of the *secunda via* of St. Thomas, where any contingent existence is equally fitted, once it is thoroughly verified, to serve as point of departure. But Descartes is not seeking the first cause of his being; he is looking for the cause of his being *in so far as he thinks the idea of God*. The other differences which he assigns between his proof and the Thomistic way are illusory or sec-

120

ondary; this one is essential and fundamental. The Cartesian proof is original, it proceeds in quite a different way from traditional proofs.

I am thought and I carry within me all the divine perfections as object of thought; they are in me *as presented,* in the idea or the portrait of the Infinite which I possess in the core of my being, that is, of my thought. Well then, have I caused myself in being? It is more difficult to give oneself being, or to overcome nothingness, than to give oneself any property whatsoever of that being. If I were the author of my being I should have given myself all those perfections—*as existing,* as real, as effectively appertaining to me—which I possess only as represented—I should have made myself God.

But, it is easy to see, I am not infinitely perfect. The One Who made me is therefore the very One whose idea I carry within me, at once the author of my being and of this idea, and Who in some way causes Himself with an infinity of perfections, by His "power so great and so inexhaustible" that He "has never needed any help in order to exist";[154] just as, if I were God, I should have caused myself with all the perfections that the idea of God presents to me—with all those perfections with which it overwhelms me. "My nature could not be what it is, that is, I should not have in me the idea of a God, if this God did not truly exist."[155]

A demonstration full of yearning, pregnant with a strange regret. Leibnitz will not be long in saying that not to be God is a *metaphysical evil.* In a clumsy effort, still cluttered up with traditional notions, Descartes has prefigured the destinies of idealism; for which in the last analysis it is a scandal that a thought which one holds to be *the* Thought should not be The Thought of Thought—itself—infinite—divine.

Many remarks could be offered here. Descartes does not admit that the only prerequisite to the proof of the existence of God by His effects should be the general notion thanks to which men agree upon the meaning of the word God,[156] and which takes the place of a nominal definition (for in this case no definition is admissible). Right from the start he finds it necessary to have the equivalent of a real definition,[157] for him the existence of God can be established only if His nature is first of all as though naturally revealed. After all, it is an idea or a representation of the divine essence itself that he needs. Why? Because, to tell the truth, even when he believes he is proving the existence of God by His effects, he does not rely upon the effects as such, he is already relying on the exigencies proper to the idea of God—itself taken as effect.

Although he does not take that opinion into account in the *Meditations,* in reality he believes in the possibility of an infinite series of causes.[158] (Furthermore he is mistaken about the thought of the Scholastics on this subject and he fancies that the *ananke stênai* arose for them from the impossibility of spanning by thought any *infinite series* whatsoever; such is not the case.[159] St. Thomas acknowledged the possibility of an endless succession of terms, he even acknowledged the possibility of a multitude infinite in act;[160] what he declared to be impossible was an infinite series of *causes* forming all together, by the present exercise of their causality, the *raison d'être* of an effect; for if there is not a first in such a series, that *raison d'être* is never constituted). Here again the idea of God present in the soul makes it unnecessary for Descartes to consider any eventual series of causes. As a matter of fact it determines from the outset a condition which the solution of the problem must meet: the cause of my being, the sought-for cause must also have the idea of the sovereign perfection—and in addition, the infinite reality which corresponds to that idea. Consequently this cause cannot be anything other than primary. I pass immediately then from myself who think God over to my cause, which is God Whom I thus think. And if one invents intermediary causes,[161] they all lead to a primary cause, not because an infinite regression in the series of *raisons d'être* is impossible, but because the primary cause is present from the beginning, represented by its idea, and demanded by it.

Descartes utilizes the traditional doctrine which looks upon things as being kept in being by the very act which creates them, but he completely distorts this doctrine, because he substitutes for the notion (metaphysical) of the contingency of perishable being his paradoxical notion (physical) of the discontinuity of time; the existence of things being consequently conceived as continually drifting into nothingness, and things constantly having to be caused anew. (Thus to the objection: what if I have always existed? he answers: some cause must be producing me continually and creating me, so to speak, over again.) After he had recognized the existence of the creator, St. Thomas proved that by the same act he creates things and preserves them all through time, because that act is untemporal, outside the whole order of time.[162] Descartes, on the contrary, before having acknowledged that a creator exists and in order to do so, takes things as continually created, because the nature of time demands that I be perpetually renewed in being. Continued creation thus becomes "the tissue of successive creations" of which Fenelon later speaks, a creation *reiterated* every instant of a time whose proper nature is misunderstood, and which is pulverized into an infinite number of indivisibles. The seventeenth century was amused over the consequences,* and wondered how the author of a crime can justly be punished if between the instant of his crime and that of his punishment he has been re-created (and an infinite number of times); has not the culprit vanished forever when the instant of his crime has passed? Did not a new man spring up out of nothingness the next moment? Here, in any case, we have the continuity of creation linked up with the (alleged) discontinuity of time and founded upon a false physical mystery instead of resting upon the metaphysical mystery of divine eternity.

Need I add that it is while setting forth this second proof that Descartes enunciates the axiom to which modern psychology owes so many pseudo-problems: "there can be nothing in our mind in so far as it is a thing which thinks, of which the mind itself has no actual awareness"?[163]

What is most important to remember, however, is the notion of God *cause of Himself* which emerges at the end of the Cartesian demonstration. The expression is of no value, although Suarez has used it: for if one can be *causa sui* in the operative order in so far as one is cause of one's own act (that is the very defintion of autonomy), how, on the contrary, in the entitative order, could a being be the cause of itself? Descartes is quite conscious of this and takes good care to state simply that God does "in some way the same thing in regard to Himself

---

* Spinoza will express indignation: . . . "Quid ergo de suo Cartesio sentit, qui statuit . . . nos singulis momentis a Deo quasi de novo creari, et nihilominus nos ex nostri arbitrii libertate agere?" **Epist. 43,** Van Vloten and Land, III, p. 160.

as the efficient cause in regard to its effect."[164] But there is much more involved here than the question of vocabulary, and it is mainly on account of its typical signification in Cartesian theodicy that this notion interests us. If I had caused myself, I should have provided myself with all the perfections of which I have the idea; that is the thread that leads the second Cartesian proof straight to God. God must therefore be conceived as an ego infinitely great Who has in this way caused Himself. In the long explanations Descartes gives to Arnauld he speaks of the *positive immensity of essence* and of the *inexhaustible power* which is "the cause or the reason for which God has no need of cause,"[165] and he confesses himself able to conceive the *by itself* of the divine privilege of existing by Himself only through the idea of efficient cause carried to the ultimate, in the way in which Archimedes demonstrated theorems on the sphere by acting *as though* the globe was a many-sided figure. These explanations to Arnauld show exactly how Cartesian thought is riveted to univocity and confuses the metaphysical analogy of the creature to the creator with an entirely different type of analogy—that of the *passage to the geometrical limit,* which causes mathematically to pass from one specific type to the other simply by increasing to infinity in the same line.

It should have been understood that the concept of *raison d'être* is analogous, and that if it formally-eminently suits God existent *by Himself,* it is not because a perfection of God, His power or His immensity of essence, is *quasi* efficient cause in regard to His being; but beyond the whole order of efficient causality, by this fact alone, that divine essence is divine existing. But one would say that Descartes sees in the affirmation of this identity only a simple analysis of concepts, without understanding that it expresses something supremely *positive*, although known at one and the same time by way of eminence and of negation. In Descartes himself the *causa sui* is orientated in the direction of libertism, and just as in us liberty is the perfection *par excellence*,[166] God is for him, above all, an infinite abyss of liberty whose good pleasure can make two-plus-one equal four, or three as He in fact wished it, or anything at all.* In Spinoza, who remains on the same level of univocity although taking up an exactly contrary position, the *causa sui* is orientated toward the pantheistic conception of a God "immanent cause" of things which have no other substantial essence than His.

THE LOGIC OF THE PERFECT

The ontological proof appears as a new absolute start of Cartesian philosophy. Nevertheless it seems that in actual fact it presented itself to Descartes' mind** as a second thought, while he was meditating upon the geometrical essences and the rational necessities they imply. Then only, and as though at the instigation of geometrical clarity, did the philosopher decide to contemplate only in its pure content and its pure intelligible exigencies that idea of God which he had until then considered in its existence and as an effect. And it is indeed noteworthy that his last proof should thus appear with a blinding flash and much more simple and compelling than the other two, in the middle of the fifth *Meditation on the essence of corporeal things.*

* See below, pp.
** It is only in the *Principles*, a pre-eminently didactic work, that it will take its logical place, which is first, among the Cartesian proofs of the existence of God. Descartes himself explained this to Burman: "Quia alia est via et ordo inveniendi, alia docendi; in *Principiis* autem docet." (Ms. of Göttingen, A.-T., V. p. 153. Cf. O. Hamelin, *Le Système de Descartes*, pp. 201-202.)

It was as though necessity demanded that the intuition of the purely geometrical nature of matter and the quasi-intuition of the existence of God should appear associated in the same sort of evidence, which gave the same weight of certitude to mechanicism as to the very existence of the Creator, and which placed the existence of the Creator on the same level of intelligibility and clarity as the most evident mathematical truths.

Is the *cogito* only a spring-board for passing over to the ontological proof, the only true beginning of philosophy? Is the *cogito* the true beginning, and the ontological proof its complement? The basic tendency of the Cartesian spirit is, to tell the truth, a yearning to join, at the extreme limit, these two absolute beginnings in a single apperception which would transcend all discourse. That limit is superhuman; we know that pure spirits know naturally, and at a single glance, themselves and God (not yet, however, God seen in His essence, but God as reflected in them). The beautiful, the strong, the dramatic thing about Descartes is that consumed by an angelic fever, he nevertheless clings to the earth and refuses, were the coherence of his system to suffer for it, to break the last ties with common sense. He knows that his *cogito* and his proof of God will never cease to be two separate processes, and that never will this proof cease to be a reasoning or change itself into an intuition.[167] The bane of modern idealism will be to try vainly to reach the limit just mentioned; it will waver between systems of the Kantian type, dominated by the *cogito* in spite of everything, and systems of the dogmatic type dominated by the ontological argument or by its substitutes.

Even though no triangle has ever existed, the idea of triangle is the idea of a certain definite nature or essence, "which is immutable and eternal, which I have by no means invented, and which in no way depends on my mind."[168] And considering what constitutes that nature I am constrained to acknowledge in it and attribute to it certain definite property, such as having the sum of its angles equal to two right angles.

Now "I find no less within myself" the idea of God "than the idea of any figure or number whatsoever." I draw it "from the treasure of my mind." It is "the idea of a supremely perfect being." But existence is a perfection, the first of all perfections; it is therefore contained in the notion of supreme perfection and required by it; it is a contradiction to assume an infinitely Perfect One which lacks the perfection of existing. By the mere logic of the Perfect then, the existence of God settles and asserts itself in human thought. "I know that an actual and eternal existence is a property of its nature no less clearly than I know that everything which I can prove about some figure or some number, belongs in truth to the nature of that figure or that number."[169]

Descartes next remarks, and quite rightly, that the case is unique. He has learned from his Scholastic masters that essence is distinct from existence in everything which is not God, and that they are identical only in God. By one of those logical dis placements so frequent in him, he wishes to make use even of this identity, a privilege of the divine nature, whose recognition at the summit of natural theology was the keystone of Christian philosophy—as a basis of departure to demonstrate the existence of God in virtue of His notion alone. "Being accustomed to make the distinction between existence and essence in all other things," the habit thus acquired leads us also to think "that existence can be separated from the essence of God, and

128

that one can thus conceive God as not actually existing." But in reality "there is no less repugnance in conceiving a God, that is to say a supremely perfect being, lacking existence, that is to say lacking in some perfection, than in conceiving a mountain which does not have a valley . . ." In the latter case one attributes to a subject an essential predicate which is not existence; in the former, and in virtue of a like necessity, one attributes to it an essential predicate which is existence itself. "It does not follow, because I cannot conceive a mountain without valley, that there is any mountain or any valley in the world, but simply that the mountain and the valley whether existent in fact or not, are inseparable from one another. Whereas by the fact alone that I cannot conceive God but as existing, it follows that existence is inseparable from Him . . ."[170]

All that is very well put; were one to weigh all the assertions just made, one could not deny any of them. And nevertheless Descartes has proved nothing. Wherein lies the sophism? Suppose we finish the incomplete phrase "By that fact alone," he says, "that I cannot *conceive God except as existing,* it follows that existence is inseparable from Him . . ."; right! the thought runs on properly although the last words are ambiguous—"and consequently," he concludes, and here is the sophism, and consequently it follows *"that He exists* veritably." No, it does not follow that the Perfect exists; it follows only that "existence" *as simply represented* is "inseparable from Him *"as simply represented,* in other words that in the object of thought: Perfect, there is of necessity the object of thought: Existence, without my having the slightest knowledge whether either object of thought truly exists.

Five centuries before Kant, St. Thomas, in pointing out the ineffectiveness of St. Anselm's argument which does not entirely coincide with the Cartesian argument, but which is of the same type, had refuted Descartes on this essential point where a *false proof* of something true was to deflect metaphysics from its course for centuries to come, and prove to be in fact as pernicious as the very negation of the same truth. We shall transpose here, relative to the Cartesian argumentation, the criticism made by St. Thomas and Cajetan of the argument of St. Anselm.

Let us admit, explains St. Thomas,[171] who does not believe in innate ideas or in ideas ready-made, let us admit that each of us, drawing from the treasure-house of his ideas, finds there as a matter of fact the idea of God as the idea of the supremely perfect being. It does not follow though, that what is presented to him by that idea exists in the nature of things, but only that it exists with an ideal existence, object of the apprehension of the mind. That existence is inseparable in the real from this supremely Perfect One can be established only if one agrees first, or establishes first, that there is in actual existence something which corresponds to the idea of the supremely Perfect.

Cajetan adds to this argument precisions of the utmost value. For it is important to recognize explicitly what Descartes has defined with such forcefulness, namely, that in the apprehension of the mind, or as an object of thought, the supremely Perfect is conceived with that perfection which is existence, I mean existence in act and in the nature of things; otherwise it would not be conceived as the supremely Perfect. In the order of representation, he writes,[172] we do not exclude any perfection, the object thus conceived has them all; but then one inevitably abstracts from existence *in actu exercito,* in exercised or lived act.

Right here is introduced the necessary distinction—key to the whole question, a distinction which Kant did not see, between existence as represented or "signified," *existentia ut significata,* and existence as effectively possessed by a subject, or as "exercised," *existentia ut exercita.* The existence I conceive among the perfections of the supreme Perfect of which I have the idea, is indeed actual existence and in the nature of things: but *ut significata,* and not *ut exercita.* It is an existence simply represented, and which remains "in the apprehension of the mind." It is an existence which I think in an idea, and not which I have the right, by that fact alone, to attribute in a judgment.

"That which is represented to the mind by the idea of the supremely Perfect," continues Cajetan (a Cajetan scarcely transposed from the lexicon of St. Anselm to that of Descartes), "is presented and thought with all perfection, even that of existence in the nature of things: but only in the quality of an object of representation, signified to the mind; and the inference from representation to existence does not hold, *a significari et cogitari ad esse non valet argumentum.*"

That the supremely Perfect "brings with it existence in the nature of things, must be understood in a double sense, namely, either in the order of exercise, or in the order of representation. In the second meaning we concede" what Descartes puts forward (but which does not prove anything); "in the first meaning, we do not. And if one were to admit it in the first sense, then without the slightest doubt this proposition [the supremely Perfect exists] would be *as self-evident* as: that which is, is."

"Now the reason why existence is not included here *in actu exercito* or as effectively possessed by a subject, but only as conceived, is that by nouns [or by ideas] things are signified as conceived; by verbs [or by judgments], as effected in existence (*ut exercitae*). That is why this statement: *existence is not,* does not imply a contradiction; but this one: *that which exists, is not,* does imply contradiction."

These brief formulas give us as it were, in passing, an arcanum of the first philosophy; Cajetan completes them in another text, where it is a question of the metaphysical perfection of the intellect being higher than that of the will:[173] the latter has as object, good—the former, being. Now good is but one with being; how then, one might ask, is the object of the intellect more immaterial, more detached from things than the object of the will? Cajetan answers: "Being itself, or *existing,* can be understood in two ways: namely, either in the effectuation of existence itself (*in actu exercito ipsius existentiae*), or as intelligible nature or object of thought (*per modum quidditatis*); and in so far as it is effectuation of existence, it adds to itself as intelligible nature. And consequently as object of the intellect it is more abstract and more purely immaterial, because it is object of the will as it is in act of effectuation of existence, but it is object of the intellect according as it constitutes in itself a certain intelligible nature (*secundum quod rationem habet quidditatis cujusdam in seipso*)."

Thus judgment and will are both opposed, although in an entirely different way, to simple intellectual apprehension. In the case of intellectual apprehension the mind grasps things, and existence itself, in the simple perspective of 'quiddities' and as intelligible values; in the case of judgment and will it refers these intelligible values to their effectuation in the extramental being (possible or actual effectuation in the case of judgment, only actual in the case of the will). Whether it be possible or actual, existence as *represented* to the mind is itself a certain intelligible value. As *effectuated* or as possessed by a subject (*ut exercita*), it adds nothing in the category of intelligible objective content or along the line of intelligible presentations and values to what it is as represented, or as an object of simple apprehension. But it does add the extra-mental position itself, the effectuation *extra causas,* to which corresponds in the mind not the simple intellectual apprehension, but either the judgment, which within the mind itself refers objects of thought to extra-mental existence as effectuable or effectuated, or the will which inclines—first within the mind itself—the subject in its entirety toward that which outside of the mind actually possesses existence.

What then, in the last analysis, is the primary root of the sophism involved in the ontological argument? St. Thomas lays it bare in the briefest of formulas: *nos non scimus de Deo quid est;* we do not know concerning God what He is in Himself;[174] to know God as He is or in His essence we should know Him intuitively; and we do not know Him thus. Consequently, to reason as Descartes does is to confound that which is "self-evident" (or immediately evident) *in itself,* and that which is "self-evident" (or immediately evident) *for us.* The existence of God is a truth of immediate evidence in itself, it is not a truth of immediatel evidence for us.[175]

This distinction is fundamental in St. Thomas; but how could it have been accepted by a system which takes as its supreme rule the adjustment of everything to the level of our reason? Such a distinction testifies drastically to the difference in level which separates intelligibility in itself from intelligibility for us.

A distinction must be made between truths immediately evident in themselves and truths immediately evident not only in themselves, but to us as well. And among these latter we must distinguish between those which are known of themselves to all of us (those concerning being in general—that is, the principle of identity and the connected principles), and those which are known of themselves to "the wise' (for example, "a pure spirit is not circumscribed in space"). In order that a truth may be known by itself (or immediately evident) *in itself,* nothing else is required than that the predicate belong to the intelligible constitutive itself of the subject.[176] But in order that it may also be immediately evident *to us,* we must be able to grasp this intelligible constitutive, plainly open before us. "Now in God, His act of existing is included in the constitutive of His essence and it follows that the existence of God is immediately evident in itself. But because the essence of God is not exposed to us, the existence of God is therefore not for us an object of immediate evidence, it requires a proof. But in the Father's house, where we shall see the divine essence, the necessity of the existence of God will be much more immediately evident to us than the principle of contradiction is at present, *multo amplius erit nobis per se notum Deum esse, quam nunc sit per se notum quod affirmatio et negatio non sunt simul verae."*[177] The existence of God is a truth known of itself to the wise of heaven. Descartes in this instance is not only of the company of pure spirits, he is of the company of the blesséd spirits.[178] The ontological argument, or rather the immediate intuition of which it is the substitute (for in beatitude there will be no further need to reason) is only valid for "the idea of God" which we shall enjoy in the vision, but then precisely there will be no more need for any idea of God; for any idea of God would remain powerless to make us see God as He is; it is not by an idea, however angelic, it is by the divine essence itself that He will be known.

In the meantime we do not see His essence, we therefore do not see in it what it necessarily implies: existence as effectively possessed, *ut exercita*. We know it by ananoetic intellection, by means of the analogous concept of being, which, like all our concepts and for the very reason that it is abstract, abstracts from existence as effectively possessed. It is not from the simple concept or from the mere notion of God, it is not by the mere unfolding of the logic of the Perfect that we know that God exists; we know it starting from existential realities grasped and affirmed in judgments (based, in the last analysis, on the experience of the senses or of consciousness), we know it starting from the existential reality of the imperfect and the finite, which bears witness that it does not suffice unto itself.

Kant clearly saw the weakness of the ontological argument and the powerlessness of a *purely* analytical process (no datum of experience pre-supposed) to reach existence itself. Unfortunately, instead of linking up that powerlessness to the conditions proper to simple apprehension and abstractive operation, he tied his criticism to an erroneous theory of existence, which derives from the nominalistic sensualism of Berkeley and Hume, and which involves his whole doctrine of concept and of judgment. For him the concept of existence is not only, like any pure concept, an empty form with no proper content; expressing no law of attribution or of subsumption, it in fact adds nothing to the subject. Existence is not a predicate. How then can he maintain that any proposition of existence is synthetic, and put existence in the table of categories? In his eyes, doubtless, a proposition of existence does nothing but duplicate the empirical existentiality included in the intuition, without clothing it with any typical function for the intellectual unification of the diverse. Be that as it may, it is fairly well known that for him there is nothing more in a hundred possible thalers than in a hundred existing thalers.

But we know that a live dog is worth more than a dead lion.[179]

The notion of existence has a content, its own intelligible value; not only is it a predicate, but a predicate which has reference to a perfection, eminent and of an order apart—actuality of every act. And if actual existence adds nothing along the line of essence and of essential predicates to the natures it actuates, it adds to them nevertheless something eminently real and intelligible, though quite outside the whole order of essence, and therefore attached to it contingently. It is not true that the concept of a hundred possible thalers is the same as that of a hundred real thalers; in the latter case there is more than in the former, although the nature or object of thought "hundred thalers" is the same in both. But in the latter there is a notional complex (the concept of thaler and the concept of real existence joined together), in the former there is only the concept of thaler; and as the notional complex "hundred real thalers" still falls under the head of the "first operation of the mind" (simple apprehension), the actual existence which it involves is nothing but existence as represented, reached in the perspective of intelligible natures or of "quiddities" (*existentia ut significata*).

If furthermore we go on to the "second operation of the mind," to judgment, and if instead of conceiving simply *a hundred real thalers,* we affirm: *there are a hundred thalers there,* the concept of thaler and that of real existence are joined in quite another way, I mean that they are then, by an original and irreducible act which is the judgment itself, jointly referred by the mind and within the mind to the way in which things behave outside the mind, and the actual existence thus affirmed is existence in the act of effectuation or as effectively possessed (*existentia ut exercita*). When reason establishes that God exists, it does not do so by extrapolating existence *ut significata* included in a notion, in order to make of it an existence *ut exercita* affirmed in a judgment—it does so by advancing from the very outset along the line of the effectuation of existence, that is to say, by starting from certain experience data where existence is apprehended *ut exercita,* in order to compound, in this very quality of existence *ut exercita,* and under the compulsion of the first principles intuitively grasped in the perception of being— to compound, I say, the notion of a first and supreme cause with that of existence, drawn from experience, by abstraction, in all its analogical amplitude.*

Refusing to see in judgment a compounding of notions (a compounding of a unique and specific type), regarding judgment as the blossoming-forth, if I may so put it, of an intuition in a concept, Kant could not see the radical difference which distinguishes simple apprehension from judgment, conception from

---

* Furthermore this compounding of subject and predicate is not attributed to God, it has only to do with our mode of knowing.

assertion. That is what vitiates his criticism of the ontological argument.

Philosophical meanderings! Descartes had upon a wrong reason rightly concluded that God exists. Kant, upon several wrong reasons, rightly condemned Descartes' proof. What is unpardonable is that he should pretend, through a sheer sophism, to have linked every demonstration of the existence of God with this false proof. Thus metaphysical presumptuousness comes full-circle. Modern metaphysics began by considering unworthy of pure thought those humbly and strongly human processes, —both flesh and spirit as we are, which, from the paradoxical intertwining of being and indigence manifest in visible things, climbed to the subsisting Being Himself. These processes were replaced by false proofs as brilliant as they were fragile. Kant himself, in 1763, was seeking, as Descartes had sought, an *a priori* demonstration, the weakness of which he was not to be long in discovering. After that the failure of these false proofs will be proclaimed. But the true proofs will not only risk being ruined along with the false; in order to make the ruin inevitable, irreparable and complete, care will have to be taken to make sure that the true have value only by virtue of the false. There is nothing left, everything is destroyed. Man lies half dead by the roadside, stripped by invisible robbers.

The sophism in question has become a sort of sacred legacy in the official teaching of philosophy, a legacy transmitted without investigation and imposed on one generation after another by a powerful effect of prestige; this sophistry is, nonetheless, visible to the naked eye. To demonstrate the existence of God by His effects, Kant explains,[180] is, in a first moment, to establish, starting from a contingent existence (mine, for example), that there exists an absolutely necessary being; and to conclude, in a second moment, that that being is God, because the absolutely necessary being is supremely perfect. Now, in the second moment, it is the ontological argument that is really brought into play. Why? Because the two propositions "any necessary being is perfect" and "any perfect being is necessary" can be considered reciprocal; they are equivalent. To say: *the absolutely necessary being is supremely perfect,* is simply to state the major premise of the ontological argument: *the supremely perfect being is absolutely necessary.* Thus the "cosmological" argument presupposes this major premise and concludes only in virtue of it— it is nothing more than the ontological argument in disguise.

But what constitutes indeed the characteristic of the ontological argument? Is it to consider as identical supreme perfection and necessary existence? Or is it to pass from a supreme perfection *conceived or represented only,* to a necessary existence *affirmed?* Kant himself proclaimed that the flaw proper to that false proof is to conclude from the ideal to the real. And now he claims to reduce to it a proof which concludes from the real to the real. From the notion of a triangle, I infer that any (Euclidian) triangle necessarily has the sum of its angles equal to two right angles, and yet I should be wrong to conclude that this property is posed in the existence in act as possessed by a subject, for I can remove from existence both the triangle and its property. But if I have begun by establishing that such a triangle exists, shall I not have the right to conclude that its property exists also?

Let us admit the equivalence of these two theses: *any supremely perfect being is absolutely necessary* and *any absolutely necessary being is supremely perfect.* What is the meaning of the first formula in the ontological argument? It means this:

any supremely perfect being MERELY REPRESENTED *exists neces-sarily* IN EFFECT. The second formula suffers from the same defect if understood in the same way: *any absolutely necessary being* MERELY REPRESENTED *exists* EFFECTIVELY *with complete perfection.*

But if I think: "it is of the notion of a supremely perfect being to be absolutely necessary," otherwise expressed: "every supremely perfect being exists with an absolutely necessity, *if it exists*"; or if I think: "it is of the notion of an absolutely necessary being to be supremely perfect," or put in another way: "any absolutely necessary being is supremely perfect, *if it exists*"—in neither case has my reasoning the least collusion with the ontological argument. And if I have begun by establishing that an absolutely necessary being *exists,* I have evidently the right to conclude that this being, of which I know that it exists, possesses a supreme perfection which also exists. It is thus that St. Thomas proceeds. Beginning not with a concept but with experience, he has first shown that the primary Cause or the primary Necessary or the primary Being or the primary Intelligence exists; and it is when assured of that existence that he concludes that such a being is pure act and infinite perfection; thus he passes from the real to the real, not at all from the ideal to the real. To claim that that is supposing the ontological argument and concluding in virtue of it is completely sophistical.

If Kant could fall into so patent a sophism, it is because in truth, according to the implications of his own system, there is a kind of ontological argument hidden in every existential assertion concerning a purely intelligible subject. By an inversion of the real order of things, judgment for Kant ends in the act of conceiving; it consists in enclosing the contents of an intuition

140

in an ideal conceptual form; it ends up in the ideal. Existential judgments of experience make us conceive in a given manner or ideally subsume a sensible matter (existing in so far as felt, not as judged). But to submit a purely intelligible subject to a judgment of existence has no meaning; it is either to place that subject in the extension of phenomena and to make something sensible of it in order to make it a thing existent, or else it is to enclose it, a simple object of concept, in an ideal form, and thus to establish oneself in the ideal order so as to remain in the purely intelligible order. And hence to claim in virtue of a connection of concepts to attribute a real predicate to a supra-sensible subject is *ipso facto* and in any case to pass from the ideal to the real.

Here we touch upon one of the primary roots of Kant's system: namely his theory of judgment and of the concept, an arbitrary presupposition resulting from a reaction against sensualistic nominalism, which reaction was itself incapable of rising above nominalism, and consequently able only to aggravate the error. If Kant had discerned the true nature of judgment he would have understood that in an existential judgment of experience, the mind, compelled by sensory intuition, declares to be identical in reality two notions, two concepts each of which has its own intelligible content; and that the intelligible content of the predicate "existing" being an essentially analogous object of thought, the mind is justified in applying this predicate, purified of all empirical significance, to purely intelligible subjects which experience, in the light of the first intellectual principles, requires as being its *raison d'être*.

THE DREAM OF DESCARTES

THE ETERNAL TRUTHS

We know that for Descartes the eternal truths are eternal from the fact that God is immutable, but that being "created truths" they are contingent in regard to the sovereign liberty of the Creator, Who could have brought it about that square circles were possible, and in which case He could have given us an understanding adapted by nature to such objects. "Those truths that are called eternal, such as that *totum est majus sua parte,* etc., would not be truths at all, had God not established it thus."[181] "It is my opinion that one cannot say of anything that it cannot be done by God; as a matter of fact, the essence of the true and the good (*omnis ratio veri et boni*) depends upon His omnipotence, and I should not dare to say that God cannot make mountains exist without valleys or one plus two be equal to three; but I say only that He gave me a mind of such nature that a mountain without a valley or a sum of one plus two not equal to three cannot be conceived by me."[182] It meant already, before the Kantian doctrine of *a priori* forms, making of intelligible necessities constraints of nature or of entitative constitution imposed by the structure of the thinking subject (whereas in reality they are precisely necessities of intelligence infinitely transcending any physical constraint; and which furnish the mind, beyond all order of fact and of the empirical, the very law and intimacy of being—of that being into which the mind is made to be transformed, immaterially, in and by the act of knowledge); it meant introducing a kind of transcendental empiricism into the core of the rational as such; and it meant evading the primordial evidence through which, attaining in extra-mental being not only certain determinations of fact but

142

certain absolute possibilities and impossibilities which this being implies by itself we are assured of thus knowing the truth which no will can abolish and the absolute necessity of which the divine intelligence perceives infinitely better than ourselves.

Descartes imagines that if the eternal truths are absolutely necessary, if God cannot bring it about that nothingness is something, that the past never existed, or that creatures do not depend upon the creator,[183] it is because these truths are independent of God and impose their necessity upon Him as upon us. He rightly says: "If men really understood the meaning of their words, they could never without blasphemy say that the truth of something precedes the knowledge that God has of it . . . One must never say therefore that *si Deus non esset nihilominus istae veritates essent verae;* for the existence of God is the first and most eternal of all possible truths . . .[184] It is as though one were to speak of God as of a Jupiter or Saturn and to make Him subject to the Styx and to the Fates, to say that these truths are independent of him.[185] But he says to conclude that everything depends upon the divine pleasure alone: "The mathematical truths which you call eternal have been established by God and depend entirely upon Him, as do all other creatures . . . Do not be afraid, I beg you, to affirm and to publish broadcast that it is God Who established these laws in nature, just as a king establishes laws in his kingdom . . . And they are all *mentibus nostris ingenitae,* just as a king would impress his laws upon the hearts of all his subjects, if he had the power to do it."[186] He has disposed the eternal truths *"in eodem genere causae* that He has created everything, that is to say *ut efficiens et totalis causa."*[187] "You ask what God did to produce them. I say that *hoc ipso quod illas ab aeterno esse voluerit et intellexerit, illas creavit,* or rather (if you attribute the word *creavit* only to the existence of things) *illas disposuit et fecit . . ."*[188]

We certainly do not say that divine intelligence depends upon the eternal truths, that it is determined by them and subject to them. The only object which specifies it is the divine essence, which is the divine intellection itself. But we do say that, seeing in that essence all the modes of participation which it admits, divine intelligence knows and determines from this fact all creatures possible and all the truths which concern them, and which are so dependent upon God that, in order for them to be changed, the essence of God itself would have to change first.

Let us here note a theological opinion of Vasquez which was strongly attacked by John of St. Thomas, and in which Vasquez defends positions very similar to those Descartes will later defend; this suggests the possibility that the latter, once more,[189] might have been in a certain historical dependence with regard to the former.

It is a question of knowing if in the very virtue of the vision of the divine essence (*ex vi visionis essentiae divinae*) the blesséd see in God possible creatures. No, Vasquez answers;[190] for if the possible creatures could be seen simply by the fact alone that God is seen, there would be a necessary connection between God and the possible creatures; and when there is a necessary connection between two terms, if one happens to cease, the other must also cease: if the possibility of the creatures should come to an end, the divine essence would also have to end. But the divine essence is so absolute and independent that even if every creature were rendered impossible, the divine essence would still continue to exist. In maintaining that by the sole fact that they see God, the blesséd see in Him possible creatures, or created truths, one makes the primary Truth dependent upon creatures . . . Are not the following lines from Descartes a faithful echo of these assertions of Vasquez? "You also ask what has forced God to create these truths; and I say that He was as free to bring about that it would not be true that all the lines drawn from the centre to the circumference were equal, as He was free not to create the world. *And it is certain that these truths are no more necessarily connected with His essence than are other creatures.*"[191]

Quite on the contrary, answers John of St. Thomas,[192] it is the transcendence and absolute independence of the divine essence that we affirm in affirming that there is a neccessary connection between the primary Truth and the possibility of things, but a necessary connection wherein the dependence is completely of the latter upon the former. The higher the cause is above its possible effects, and the more independent it is with regard to them, the more supremely is it mistress of them, subjecting to itself their whole being: and consequently is it the more perfect means of knowing them in their very dependence in its own regard as it makes them what they are. If the eternal truths cannot cease without the primary Truth ceasing to be, it is because they are so dependent upon the primary Truth that in order to do away with them, the primary Truth itself must be abolished. Thus it is that in order to destroy a conclusion necessarily deduced, one must first destroy the more certain and higher truth of the principles; and that, not because the truth of the principles would depend upon the truth of the conclusions, but because the latter, on the contrary, depends upon the former.

"Although the possibility of creatures is, as regards its object, *formally* a created truth, receiving from God what it is and therefore inferior to Him, nevertheless it is *radically* the divine truth itself, because the root of the possibility of creatures is God.

" . . . The formal possibility of creatures cannot be annihilated unless one begins by annihilating the radical possibility, because that formal possibility is not something real outside of God; if a reality which is not God, is given in fact, it is because it is produced, and in this case one would not have only possibility, but existence of creature. The formal possibility of creatures is therefore only an absence of self-contradiction and an extrinsic denomination resulting from the radical and active possibility which is in God. And an extrinsic denomination can only be suppressed and cease in the object which receives it if one begins by suppressing the real form from which that denomination comes, as 'to be seen' can cease for an object only if the act of vision which is in the eye first ceases . . ."

Thus is explained and justified, *in via judicii,* in the synthetic and descending order,[193] our unchallengeable certitude, first gift of the first light risen in us, and present in us from the beginning, that the principle of identity and the other first principles and every intelligible necessity and every essential and non-temporal truth bear our intelligence to the very heart of the possible or impossible in itself, of the creatable or the non-creatable, and so admit it, however weak its mode of conceiving may be, into that very universe of the pure possibles which, in contemplating His essence God knows and determines eternally, in virtue of the proper necessity of His being. In order to abolish the principle of identity, as to abolish the possibility of an ant, one would first be obliged to abolish the divine essence. The eternal truth of this principle does not depend upon divine will and creative freedom, it depends upon divine necessity, I mean upon the knowledge that God necessarily has of His infinitely necessary essence, knowledge which bears for that very reason upon all that is possible and creatable, not, of course, as upon a specifying object, but as upon an object specified and materially attained.

We may note here that with regard to *possible* creatures and their relations to God, Spinoza is right, or at least would be right, if the boundless ocean of *natura naturata*—I mean of all the creatable (not yet willed, or loved or existent)—derived from *natura naturans* not by way of immanence and as expression of what *natura naturans* is, but by way of transcendence, as a possible, and irremediably inadequate participation in or imitation of that which saturates with knowledge this *natura naturans* which is an *intelligentia intelligens,* determining in virtue of its own necessity all the possibles it knows. Spinoza's essential error is to confuse with the pure possible or the creatable, which is nothing outside of God, the created and the existent, which as such is willed, loved, chosen. Thus he wrongs the divine freedom.

Descartes' error is quite the opposite; he confuses the creatable and the possible with the created; then everything, I mean all the laws of essences, the distinction between being and non-being, between the intelligible and the absurd, between good and evil, falls under the pure will and the liberty of a supreme Arbitrary; Descartes wrongs the wisdom, the intelligence of God. St. Thomas, departing from his customary serenity, considers it blasphemy to make good and evil dependent upon the pure will of God: "To say that justice depends upon the pure and simple will of God is to say that the will of God does not proceed according to the order of His wisdom, which is blasphemy."[194]

One would say that Descartes mistook the meaning of the

147

word created truth. The eternal truths are created truths because they have bearing upon the very creatability of things—which has no reality whatsoever outside of God, as John of St. Thomas explained it above. Descartes speaks of them as though they were created things. In so doing he falls into an anthropomorphic illusion which makes him believe that if they are necessary even for God, it is because God presumably depends upon them as we depend upon them. In addition he seems to assume a presupposition on the nature of the object of thought as such, or, in Scholastic language, of the *esse objectivum seu cognitum,* which it would be important to detect and which would deserve special historical studies.[195] Everything happens as if for Descartes the idea of an essence or of a possible were the image of a duplicate which of course does not exist, but which nevertheless, being something real, is not completely non-existent. Had not the Scotists admitted for the object known as such and particularly for the possibles eternally known of the divine intelligence, a sort of *esse diminutum* intermediary between the real being and the *ens rationis,*[196] the merely ideal entity? Does not Leibnitz in his turn speak of the competition and struggle between the possibles? According to the presupposition we are discussing, a sort of mathematician's Platonism of which Descartes never perhaps became aware, the ideal would thus be endowed with I know not what beginning or virtuality of existence. One would then understand how the philosopher can consider the eternal truths as creatures, as things that God has made, like eternal models which He supposedly traces, and which have in His thought, as it were, a sort of created existence.

But if the eternal truths are created and contingent with regard to God as is everything which is created, how is it they are immutable from the fact that God is immutable? The immutability of the creator does not pass on to the creatures, and it is in His very immutability that He regulates and causes their changes. Descartes is here guilty of a strange inconsistency, which is all the more serious as we come across it in reference to realities as authentically created as movement and the quantity of movement. If the quantity of movement remains constant, it also is because God does not change.[197] Here we have one of those recoils so frequent in Descartes. His metaphysics of the eternal truths carried him exactly contrary to Spinoza, but his metaphysics of the laws of movement clears the way to Spinozism, the fundamental law of a created reality like movement is deduced now from the properties of the divine nature. But did not the metaphysics of eternal truths itself hide something else, which Spinoza would also turn to account? If Descartes attaches so much importance to it, it is because it frees physics utterly from the parasitic anxiety about finality, for the decisive reason that in reality there are no final causes[198]—God does not act for aims, nor does He ordinate things to one another as means to ends, because for His will there is no order of wisdom to be followed, because in Him there is no *virtual* distinction (depending on our mind alone, but grounded in reality) between intelligence and will,[199] because He acts by pure efficiency of freedom. For Spinoza He acts by pure efficiency of nature;[200] the *per intellectum et verbum* absolutely essential to divine action has been eliminated for the benefit of a simple necessity of nature. Descartes had already sacrificed it, or clouded it over, for the benefit of will.

THE DREAM OF DESCARTES

THE DIFFICULTIES OF UNIVOCITY

The poverty of Descartes' theodicy has often been noticed. Once having proved the existence of the infinite and supremely perfect being, the philosopher hurries over the questions concerning divine nature with a somewhat embarrassed haste. He is manifestly interested only in those divine attributes upon which he rests his metaphysics and his physics, and which he finds useful in founding science: in particular the veracity of the Perfect, His liberty, His immutability. God, in Descartes' philosophy as even more generally in the cultural forms of our classical age, is as though withdrawn into heaven, where He is no longer anything more than the supreme and inscrutable Guarantee of nature and of science, of the power and the felicity which reason must conquer, and of the "citizenship" which we definitely intend to carry out, in spite of St. Paul, not *in coelis* but *in terra.* Hence the anguish and suffering of a Pascal, who saw these things—and who had very good reasons for "not forgiving" Descartes.

Moreover, the problems of natural theology could not exert a very powerful appeal to a man who was determined to devote only a few hours a year to metaphysics. But a much more profound reason must have intervened here. If, in approaching such problems, one is looking everywhere for the quick and the easy, and for geometrical clarities, one risks falling inadvertently into the shadows and the fancies of anthropomorphism. That is what happened to Descartes without his knowing it. But the very instinct of science is antipathetic to anthropomorphism, a certain embarrassment secretly warns the mind of the vulgarity from which it then suffers, and the snares to which it is exposed. The more it gives way to anthropomorphism the more it wearies

150

of theodicy and seeks to evade the problems it has lost the taste for solving. Or else, as soon as it becomes aware of the anthropomorphic character of what it attributes to God, it will deny the divine attribute instead of amending its conception of it.

Cartesian thought is not anthropomorphic in its knowledge of the world, where mathematics tends to free it* from all subjection to human imagery; for want of the metaphysical instrument of analogy which alone frees metaphysics from that subjection, it is incurably anthropomorphic in its knowledge of God. It is because he conceives of God as a human monarch raised to the absolute that Descartes attributes every law of things to His good pleasure alone—and in Malebranche himself, who is not Cartesian on this point, and whose philosophy presents itself as an explicit protest against anthropomorphism, the glory of God will still remain a sublimation of the glory of human kings. An anthropomorphic imagery is also, as we have seen, in the background of the notion of God *causa sui* and of the Cartesian theory of eternal truths. And we may well marvel at the way univocity contrives at one moment to have what one affirms badly conceived, at another to deny what has been badly conceived. Descartes affirms that God is eternal, but it is an endless time that he thus attributes to Him.[201] He refuses to attribute to God our human way of pursuing an end, but in the last analysis, it is in order to deny that God disposes to an end the things which He does;[202] which is nevertheless the characteristic of any intelligent agent.

In a general way Cartesian knowledge of divine perfections

---

* It is true that there is still a strong dose of anthropomorphism in mechanicism, especially in Cartesian mechanicism. But what we mean to say is that a formally mathematical physics *tends* by nature to free itself of all anthropomorphic residue.

proceeds in a purely geometrical fashion: God being by definition the supremely perfect, nothing is more simple than to attribute to Him everything which it seems to us to be a perfection to possess[203]—without the slightest critical elaboration of the concepts which we thus use, without that attribution being therefore justified or comprising any sure criterion (in this way Malebranche will add intelligible extension to the list of divine excellences); and without the possibility of any philosophical solution being proposed to the apparent antinomies and to the essential questions which concern the divine nature and operations. Not only does natural theology find itself stripped of its weapons and wretchedly impoverished, but in addition God is thought of, in reality, only as the sum or the integral of all human perfections raised such as they are to the absolute; and the divine simplicity, upon which Descartes is so insistent, is itself for him only a univocal simplicity in which he cannot recognize the transcendent foundation of our ideal distinctions. It cannot be otherwise where an authentic doctrine of analogy is lacking. From this point of view one must say that Cartesianism, in respect to Christian metaphysics elaborated during the preceding centuries, has been one of the most singular regressions that the history of thought has had to record. T. L. Penido's remarks find there an eminent application: "Analogical similitude such as the philosopher considers it . . . is not [like that which the naturalist studies most of the time] the unequal participation in the same generic or specific perfection, but a resemblance in relationships, connecting diverse essences. It is of crucial interest to note that it is by means of this pseudo-analogical gradation that the slipping toward anthropomorphic univocity is most often produced in theology. One takes a created perfection, one increases it indefinitely along the same line and one says: there is the 'way of eminence' (attributing to God, the perfections we know here on earth raised to the nth power), divine perfection is at the end. The error here is complete; that is not metaphysics, that is physics; it is quantitative theology . . ."[204] Because of their essentially analogical nature it is not along the same line (of the created term of the analogy), it is along another line, that of the pure act, that transcendental perfections demand to pass on to the absolute. In this case a metaphysics of the divine reality is possible.

But let us try to discover the roots of Cartesian theodicy. Let us recall how the Cartesian proofs of the existence of God proceed. The first two necessarily presuppose that the idea of God is the "most clear and distinct of all our ideas." And as to the third, in what sense is it valid? It also presupposes, necessarily, that the idea of God is not one of those materially false ideas whose phantom threatens the great undertaking of the philosopher. And how are we assured of that? In actually contemplating it. We must not look away from it for a single instant (otherwise the Mischievous Genius might turn up); on that condition it enables us to pass directly to the necessary existence of Him Who alone can exorcise the Mischievous Genius, and by Whom certitude is founded forever. But this is because in contemplating it in actuality we are subdued by its internal clarity; we see that it is "the image of a true and immutable nature."[205]

When he wondered whether the idea of God would not be a pseudo-idea like that of the rhombus inscribed in the circle, Descartes clearly foresaw the Leibnitzian objection.[206] (Historians do not always deal justly with him on this point.) Yet he brushed it aside at once, and not by means of a proof like the one Leibnitz later (vainly) attempted: but by the very experience and the sole experience of the evidence and of the intelligible consistence of that idea.[207] If for him the existence of God is provable, and is not self-evident, on the other hand His possibility is self-evident—through the idea of Him—like the existence of the geometrical essences. "Possible existence is contained in the notion or the idea of all those things which we conceive clearly and distinctly."[208] And Descartes goes on to add in defense of his third proof against the objections of Caterus: "If I picture to myself a triangle or a square (I cannot speak here of the lion or the horse, because their natures are not entirely known to us), then certainly all the things I recognize as being contained in the idea of the triangle . . . I can state with truth concerning the triangle itself; and of a square, everything which I find to be contained in the idea of the square."[209] *I cannot speak here of the lion or the horse, because their natures are not entirely known to us:* a treacherous parenthesis! Is the divine nature itself then "entirely known" to us (that is, known to the specific degree) like the nature of geometrical essences? The ontological proof is valid only if it bears upon a nature which is given to us through our idea of it as clearly and as distinctly, as evidently, as "completely" as the mathematical natures. The idea of God is really dealt with by Descartes, as we remarked earlier, as if it revealed to us the divine essence in itself. It is impossible more violently to affirm the univocity of being (and particularly, in this case, of the perfect), the root principle of the surface anthropomorphism pointed out above. Among metaphysicians less off-hand than Descartes and less indifferent to metaphysics, this same root of univocity, in virtue of a much more profound logic, will put forth another branch equally inimical to divine transcendence: the ontologism of Malebranche, or the Spinozian doctrine of the unique substance . . .

Here is where the drama of Cartesian anthropomorphism begins. Descartes is unconscious of his anthropomorphism, and he does not wish to be either an ontologist or a pantheist; as he claims to keep, in his doctrine of the soul and the body, the traditional conclusions concerning the unity of the human compound (with principles which completely disrupt this unity), likewise in theodicy he claims to retain the traditional conclusions concerning the transcendence of divine reality with regard to the very idea which we use in order to know that reality. How are these conclusions to be preserved in spite of everything? "To understand," he explains, "is to embrace with thought; but to know a thing, it is sufficient to touch it with thought."[210] A mountain cannot be embraced but it can be touched. All very well; but the question is precisely to know *how* such a comparison can be applied to our knowledge of God: in the immensity of divine essence is there something which we can reach directly, by a clear and distinct idea revealing the possibility of its object, the rest remaining out of reach? Such a completely spatial and quantitative conception would be absurd. And the philosopher is constrained to acknowledge that "every time I have said that God could be known clearly and distinctly, I have never meant to imply anything more than that finite knowledge, adjusted to the small capacity of our minds."[211] A diplomatic reply, des-

155

tined merely to brush aside an importunate question, a theologian's chicanery?

The problem is much more serious: Descartes must not only safeguard an apparent agreement with traditional Christian teaching; it is his innermost thought, an essential part of his own doctrine which is at stake here. If his deduction concerning divine attributes is anthropomorphic, it is entirely in spite of himself; anthropomorphism is repugnant to the most personal susceptibilities of his philosophical sense, and the idea of reducing divine incomprehensibility to the measure of man horrifies him. And not only does he know that God is incomprehensible, he knows it, as it were, by definition. "It is of the nature of the infinite that I who am finite and limited am not able to understand it."[22] But in good logic of clear ideas, can I even conceive it? Here bursts forth the antinomy which Descartes would never see; it is due to the very notion of the idea of God as image of the Infinite, or object seen in thought and representing the Infinite—and not as analogically elaborated starting from experience and from the notion of finite being, but as given from the very beginning, before the idea of the finite, and entirely positive. Descartes reasons on that idea—a faithful and valid picture in his opinion—as though it had an infinite "objective being." But as a picture painted in us, a created idea, its "objective being" cannot be otherwise than created and finite: and therefore how could it be a true image of the Infinite, which can help us to know it?[213]

We observed in the preceding chapter, moreover, that science for Descartes develops by reducing analytically what there is to know to ideas clear and distinct in themselves, that is to say, to atoms of evidence, and by binding these atoms of evidence to one another by means of a succession of intuitions which replaces syllogism. Instead of a conclusion which falls under the evidence of the principles, we now have objects of intuition which fall under the evidence of the idea, or of simple apprehension, and no knowledge is possible except of such objects. In other words, in following to the very end this line of thought, what is not contained in the grasp of our understanding, what is beyond our ideas, cannot give occasion to any knowledge. Let no one trouble himself then, in disputes about the Infinite![214] The world is infinite in extent, matter is infinitely divided. God is infinite. Let us accept these assertions as necessary without trying to examine that infinite which they bespeak. The idea of the infinite is not workable for reason, nothing can be got from it, it resists rational treatment. Infinite God! Incomprehensibe God! It is to a God absolutely obscure and shadowy for us, to a God upon Whom it would be supremely rash for us to try to focus the gaze of our reason, that are appendant the crystal chains of clear ideas and human science, delegated to know the finite, to know only the finite. Right here is the secret root which explains the indigence of Descartes' theodicy. Here lies the deep instinct of agnosticism, which, immanent in Cartesian thought, counterbalances the other instinct, the instinct of univocity. But do two extremely opposing errors cancelling one another make a true philosophy? And if the infinite thus completely eludes reason, how do we know that the infinite being exists?

Suppose we try to push our attempted exegesis a step further. We know that for Descartes our concepts do not all resolve into the single primordial concept of being; there is an irreducible plurality of simple natures, each one known by an immediately clear and distinct idea. The idea of the infinite is one of these absolutely primary ideas. That is why, as Descartes sees it, it is as absurd to suppose that the idea of the finite precedes the idea of the infinite, as to suppose that the idea of non-being precedes the idea of being. For him, this idea of the Infinite is a primordial datum. Descartes never became aware of the above noted antinomy concerning it. Immediately clear and distinct (in so far as we conceive clearly that what is infinite is boundless), but like a monolith within us, it cannot enter into any chain of deductions; that is its special prerogative. No question is to be raised which would lead to a rational explicitation of the object of which it is the image. A question can be raised nevertheless concerning the cause of the presence in our thought of the idea of the absolutely infinite being.

But on the other hand there is within us another absolutely primary idea, that of the supremely perfect being. (That these two absolutely first ideas, the idea of the Infinite and that of the Perfect, which do not postulate any common idea into which they resolve, should be the image of the same object, cannot be demonstrated by Cartesian logic unless this logic be untrue to itself. In reality, it assumes it gratuitously.) Now here, for Cartesian logic an analytical process is possible: in virtue of the identity between being and perfection, the perfect establishes itself, so to speak, in existence. And it is here, in the perspective of the idea of the perfect, that a deduction from divine attributes is possible.

Thus appears, in the final analysis, a Cartesian theodicy with a double centre of gravity; this theodicy, along the line of the idea of the infinite, would tend, except for the affirmation of the very existence of God, toward equivocity and agnosticism, and along the line of the idea of the perfect, it would tend toward univocity and ontologism.

Whether or not one accepts this interpretation, the contradiction remains at the heart of the system. In order that I may know God exists, the idea of God must be one of those clear and distinct ideas that my mind sees, feels and handles as its own possession—one of those ideas which by virtue of their evidence provide it with the essence of their object. Then Descartes will speak of an intuitive grasping of the intellectual nature through which he attains, at once, himself in the *cogito* and God in the idea of God.[215] And on the other hand, in order to have God remain God, He must be obscurity itself for my knowledge and my ideas.

Descartes swings from one term of the antinomy[216] to the other. He still holds the two ends of the chain, but there is no longer any chain; he himself has broken it. That is the tragedy of his philosophy, as of any anthropomorphic and imaginative theodicy. It conceives an image of God which is that of the creature enlarged to the infinite. *Absit!* Then it hastens to cover that image with a thick cloud of agnosticism. Such are these solid clouds of dizzying scrolls which baroque sculpture spreads over the figures of the beyond, in which what one manages to see retains an irremediably profane aspect, and which one can worship only by hiding them.

What Descartes felt to be true, he unfortunately did not know how to establish. Let us fall back on our idea of the infinite; it bears witness to the power of disengaging from sensible and imaginable being an analogous and transcendental notion of being —a notion free from all the sensible, and valid beyond it; and from then on, in seeking from what supreme source this very power and our act of thought are derived and upon what supreme principle in being they depend, we must acknowledge the existence of a primary being which is intellection in pure act. Let us consider likewise the idea of the supremely perfect being; it refers our thought to beings—and to our own being—which exist when nevertheless in so many respects they are not; and how could such beings exist if the self-subsisting Being did not exist? But these are not the specifically Cartesian proofs. Perceived in one swift movement of reason they are the ever-known ways from the visible to the invisible, which find their full metaphysical and critical elucidation only in the rational technique prepared by the great mediaevals.

Cartesian idealism did not build up a theodicy, it imagined one, brilliant, incoherent and invulnerable, like great edifices in a dream. Rationalism dreams a great deal; because reason left to itself asks only to sleep the sleep of the senses. It stirs in its sleep; the flash of a human glance gleams on the side of a heap of torpor, that the mischievous genii weary with illusions. If Christian philosophy remains more awake, if in it reason comes out of the shadows of "admirable science" to adhere to the real with all its strength, it is because an ardor for being far sharper than the ardor which springs from reason's sole resources inwardly stimulates it.

CHAPTER V

THE CARTESIAN HERITAGE

CHAPTER V

THE CARTESIAN HERITAGE

NOTE: The report we made at the Franco-Russian Studio the 27th of January, 1931, on *Descartes and the Cartesian Spirit,* seemed to us to bring the preceding studies to a natural conclusion. That is why we are publishing it here, begging the reader to pardon the repetitions made inevitable by such a condensation. (The complete report of the Franco-Russian Studio meeting appeared in *Cahiers de le Quinzaine,* Paris, February 1931.)

I

"During this long period of time [thirty centuries], five or six men stand out as having thought and created ideas; and the rest of the world has worked upon these thoughts . . . In the barbaric centuries of the Occident, [philosophy] has been nothing but an absurd and insensate jargon sanctified by fanaticism and worshipped by superstition . . . From the time of Aristotle until the time of Descartes, I perceive a vacuum of two thousand years . . . In that general torpor, a man was needed who would again raise up mankind, who would add new vigor to understanding, a man who would have enough daring to overthrow, enough genius to reconstruct; a man who . . ." a man that . . . "That man must have been Descartes."

Thus did Thomas express himself in 1765, in his *Eloge académique de Descartes.* And we might say that official French teaching has been of Thomas's opinion up to the recent works on mediaeval thought by which Mr. Etienne Gilson opened the eyes of the Sorbonne.

163

THE DREAM OF DESCARTES

Ought I too, by way of introduction, to sing the praises of Descartes? After all, to be the adversary of a philosopher does not mean that one underestimates his genius. It is commonplace to state the fact that Descartes was a philosopher of genius, a superbly headstrong intelligence, heroic in his way, one of those great people whose thought engenders a world; and, in addition, an admirable initiator and creator in the domain of the physical and mathematical sciences (a necessary condition for his historic task). I should prefer briefly to outline that which, in his work, seems to me to answer the prayer of history, and to satisfy a fundamental need of the growth of thought.

On one hand, the moment which had been prepared by the Parisian Doctors in the fourteenth century, by da Vinci, and finally by Galileo the contemporary of our philosopher, the moment I say, had arrived to define the physico-mathematical science of the sensible world according to its own value, and to demand its right of free status: this in itself was a perfectly normal technical progress of knowledge, whatever the philosophical excesses it may have occasioned.

On the other hand, another moment of growth was to consist in a progress of reflection, in a turning back of thought upon itself, becoming more explicitly aware of itself and its own problems. This also was a normal moment in the evolution of the mind; a progress, not necessarily in inner perfection of philosophy, for the reflective philosophy of the ancients is more profound than that of the moderns, although they did not set it apart upon a pedestal; but rather a progress in the status and, as it were, in the morphology of philosophy.

Those are the two historical postulations whose urgency fomented the thought of Descartes' time. These desires could of themselves, and should have been realized in the pure order of reason and truth. They were in fact realized with the help of irrational forces, and with the assistance of the energies of error.

In Descartes' time the history of the sciences was blocked by the appalling somnolence of a scholasticism which had been marred by its own self-satisfaction, by pedagogical routine, and by recourse to authority. The great philosophical tradition of humanity had as active defenders scarcely anything more than the decrees of Parliaments and the gendarmes of the king. In another respect, all the ferments of intellectual anarchy set free by the humanism of the Renaissance and by the naturalist, occultist and pantheist philosophies were bringing pressure to bear against Aristotle.

Descartes, by a master-stroke, made spiritualism and the new philosophy of nature interdependent. This spiritualism, which claimed to be beating all the records, was spoiled by over-weening confidence: it was making an angel of the soul. This new philosophy of nature was spoiled by the illusion that it possessed an exhaustive knowledge of the essence of bodies, an illusion which accounts for the prestige of the mechanistic conception of the world.

Thus we see the ambivalence of the Cartesian revolution. It is advisable to distinguish the normal developments of the history of thought and the aberrant forms which Cartesianism imposed upon them.

I think that my position is thus sufficiently defined. I shall not go back over the progress—not specifically Cartesian—that Cartesian philosophy conditioned. What I should like now to do is to speak of the particular significance for modern culture of that philosophy, and of the rôle and value of the ideas infused by Descartes into that culture. I hope I may be pardoned the inevitably summary nature of the reflections I am about to propose, and which, to be suitably developed and qualified, would necessitate long and complicated explanations.

II

The most deep-seated characteristic of the Cartesian reform is more than anything else, in my opinion, one of disjunction and rupture. St. Thomas brings together, Descartes cleaves and separates, and this in the most violently dogmatic way.

The most apparent of these cleavages, the most obvious for the public at large, the least typical for the philosopher, is the break with intellectual tradition. A classical platitude shows us Descartes confronting authority with evidence, at the birth of individualism in modern philosophy.

In reality he himself would have detested that individualism. What he wanted was to be the Aristotle of the modern era and to reign forever over the Schools. On the other hand, Cartesianism has nothing of an absolute beginning about it—it is in continuity with Scholasticism.

Yes—that is perfectly true. But Descartes' continuity with Scholasticism, with a Scholasticism itself considerably abased, is, indeed, a *material* continuity. In the order of *formal* and decisive characteristics, he breaks with it, completely reversing its movement of thought. And the fact remains that the example he gave of making a clean sweep and finding out everything by himself all over again (supposedly by himself alone) is the part of his work best retained by his successors. He has not been the

Aristotle of the modern schools—not at all. But every modern philosopher is a Cartesian in the sense that he looks upon himself as starting off in the absolute, and as having the mission of bringing men a new conception of the world.

*

*   *

What was it that gave Descartes the strength to break with an age-long tradition which, hardened and brittle as it might be, had still a certain solidity, at least a social one? In other words— but the same question—what was the spiritual germ, the central intuition which must have contained, in the virtual and dynamic state, all the energies of the Cartesian revolution?

The notes made by the philosopher in his youth enable us to answer that question with a certain degree of probability. This vital and spiritual germ was the revelation of the "admirable science"—*scientia mirabilis*—that Descartes received at the age of twenty-three, during that famous dream of the tenth of November 1619—the dream he regarded as being entirely supernatural, and which decided his philosophical vocation.

It is very embarrassing for modern rationalism to have been born in a dream, and at that, in a dream which a "Genius" that had for several days past been exciting enthusiasm in him, had (according to Baillet's report) predicted to the philosopher before he had retired to his bed. However, that is the fact.

There has been much discussion of that *admirable science.* As Gaston Milhaud has proved, it was not yet the great mathematical discovery of analytical geometry, nor was it the idea of a general Algebra or universal mathematics—it was, in my opinion, much more than that. It was the idea of a universal

167

science, single and alone; one of the very unity of the under-standing; wholly mathematical in type; pre-existent in the clear ideas that thought discovers in its own inner recesses and which it has only to enumerate and regulate methodically. A strange reversal of the idea of science! In place of a specific plurality of *human* sciences, of paltry man-sciences, each one pre-supposing a development and a laborious and aristocratic perfecting of the intelligence (what we call a habitus), each having its own type of intelligibility—in place of all that, we have one single knowl-edge: science, Science with a capital 'S,' Science such as the modern world was to worship it; Science in the pure state, radi-ating from unique and unparalleled geometric clarity, and that Science is the human mind. The idea of mathematical Gnosis, the idea of universal method, the idealistic conception of knowl-edge, all that fused in one identical apperception—such, it seems to me, is the primordial vision which assigned to Descartes his destiny, on that November night when the Spirit of Wisdom, as he says in his diary, descended upon him to take possession of him, and to open to him the treasure of all the sciences.

The understanding becomes an absolute, and this absolute understanding *is* man himself.

III

What fruits did this germ bring forth? To determine them one would have to survey the whole of Descartes' system. I shall here confine myself to three principal aspects of it; the first, which concerns the connection between thought and being; the second, the intellectual hierarchies and the meaning of knowl-edge; the third, the conception of man.

THE CARTESIAN HERITAGE

From the first point of view, it is idealism that we owe to Descartes; from the second, it is rationalism; from the third, Cartesian dualism.

*

*   *

If it is the question of the connection between thought and being, I shall simply recall (in order not to become involved in discussions of too-technical a nature)—that for the Scholastics we communicate with things first by means of the senses which attain the thing itself existing outside of us, not in its intimate nature but in its action upon us; and then by means of the intellect and of ideas—ideas which are drawn actively from the senses by the mind, and which are essentially immaterial *means,* living and vital relations by which we get at what things *are,* at their natures.

Thus, whereas divine knowledge precedes things and measures them, since it makes them, our own knowledge is measured by things; and the least thing, the tiniest grain of wheat is a resisting, consisting, subsisting reality, the intellibility of which we shall never have ceased to drain.

For Descartes, on the contrary, the senses have no knowledge value; they have only a pragmatic value. And ideas are not only means, they are already *things;* it is as *things* that they are attained by thought (now conceived only as self-consciousness)— as if they were pictures which it discovers in itself. Locke's formula: *ideas are the immediate objects of thought,* is a pure Cartesian formula. Idea-pictures, idea-screens. In short, we know only our ideas; thought has direct contact only with itself.

Descartes, no doubt, does not stop there. He still believes in things, he wants to know them. You know to what device he has recourse in order to justify that knowledge. *Cogito,* my thought seizes upon itself and grasps its own existence. In this thought there is the idea of God; from the idea of God I conclude that God exists: God existing and being veridical, the clear and distinct ideas which I find in me, like innate pictures and like objects immediately attained by my thought, these idea-pictures are good; back of them are models, doubles, which are things. Thus I am certain that this table exists, and I am sure of the truth of the propositions that I can set forth on the subject because, first of all, I am sure of my thought and sure of the existence of God, through Whom I must pass in order to be sure of anything; and Who is the Guarantor of my science, of the Science.

There you have the Cartesian circuit. Modern philosophy will not be long in pulling it to pieces—from that point of view it is like the primitives according to Freud; it has killed and eaten its father, it has devoured Descartes. It is clear, for example, that the whole system remains in the air, because one simply does not demonstrate the existence of God by starting with the sole idea of God.

What is left then, is not the Cartesian system, it is the Cartesian conception of thought and ideas. Whether one believes in the existence of things as Descartes himself believed (thanks to the circuit in question), or as Spinoza did (to the extent that he was a realist) in saying that there is a parallelism between the thing and the idea, and that the order and the connection of ideas are identical to the order and connection of things, the fact remains that the modern conception of knowledge itself is from the very outset idealistic.

THE CARTESIAN HERITAGE

Thought directly attains only itself; it is not ruled by things, but by its own internal exigencies; it does not depend on things but on itself alone. A world shut up, absolute—by itself alone it develops science within itself, without measuring its strength against any extraneous resistance. There it is, a human knowledge like divine knowledge, a knowledge which depends only upon itself. When the great modern idealists, Kant and his successors, make their appearance, they will make the Cartesian root produce its natural fruit.

What is the cultural significance of idealism? It carries along with it a sort of anthropocentric optimism of thought. Optimism, because thought is a god who unfolds himself, and because things either conform to it, or do not even exist apart from it. What drama could possibly occur? Either there is no being to set off against thought, or there is only being completely docile to thought. An optimism which is anthropocentric, because the thought in question is the thought of man; it is around human thought that objects revolve. All is well for that thought; and all will be better and better.

But this optimism is, if I may say so, committed to suicide; for it presupposes a rupture with being, and finally, in spite of Descartes' personal intentions and in spite of the efforts of his immediate successors, it supposes an eviction of the ontological. There we have the great, the primordial Cartesian break. Man shut up within himself is condemned to sterility, because his thought lives and is nourished only upon the things that God has made. Man the centre of an intelligible universe which he has created in his own image, himself loses his centre of gravity and his own consistence, for his consistence is to be the image of God. He is in the middle of a desert.

*
*   *

Let us consider now another aspect of the Cartesian revolution, the aspect which concerns the intellectual hierarchies and the meaning of knowledge.

Human reason is Reason in itself, Reason in its pure state. A universal rule and measure, all things must be adjusted to its level. It is no longer measured, it measures, it subjugates the object. Even the adversaries of rationalism like Pascal have, in the seventeenth century, this absolutist conception of reason. Descartes formulated its philosophy.

Descartes did not invent evidence as textbooks believe, but he completely changed the meaning of the word. Evidence is no longer a property of the thing; that is, its radical intelligibility blossoming in the mind and imposing itself on us in the judgment we brng to bear upon the thing.[217] It becomes a property of the ideas, of the idea-pictures which we contemplate in our thought. There are self-evident ideas; they are clear and distinct ideas, the ideas of what Descartes called simple natures. To know is to reduce everything to these clear and distinct ideas, to break up the object into these atoms of evidence.

In reality, we are not born with those atoms of evidence in us. The clear and distinct ideas will, in fact, be easy ideas, the most conveniently manageable and communicable representations, the elements of a mechanical reconstruction of reality. We can see how from the Cartesian *short-cut* for arriving at wisdom people will pass on to the philosophy of enlightenment.

THE CARTESIAN HERITAGE

We can see especially how it was that evidence, for the ancients, being in the last analysis the manifestation of a mystery (that is, of the root intelligibility of created things imposing itself on our mind by becoming luminous within it), a sort of natural relationship existed for them between intelligence and mystery. On the one hand then, in order to avoid the absurd and to remain faithful to the very first evidence—that of sense perception and that of the principle of identity, science itself and philosophy had to recognize a mystery of relative unintelligibility or ontological obscurity in things: that is, potentiality in Aristotle's meaning of the word, witnessing that the created is not God, Who is the pure Act of intelligibility.

On the other hand, human knowledge had to recognize at the summit of things, a mystery of superintelligibility, that of the spiritual realities and above all, of God. And if God revealed to us in the obscurity of faith something of Himself, the intellect could and even should make every effort to penetrate as far as possible these revealed truths, and to grasp their concatenation, even though it cannot have the evidence of their principles. A science of the mysteries is possible: a science of what is not evident for us, but is infallibly believed on the authority of the first Truth—that is theology. And Christian intelligence could say with St. Lawrence: "My night allows the light to enter," *mea nox obscurum non habet.*

Thus the whole movement of intelligence was holy, consecrated, because it was orientated toward God. Philosophy itself was Christian, secular knowledge was Christian. As a matter of fact, philosophy by its very object is quite distinct from faith and from theology. It is strictly of the natural and rational order. But in the subject, in the human soul, it is fortified and

173

illuminated by the superior virtues with which it is in vital continuity, integrated to the great movement of love which carries the soul toward the vision of its Creator.

With Descartes, everything changes. This distinction achieved in coherence and dynamic solidarity becomes separation, isolation—and soon even opposition. Philosophy is sufficient absolutely and unto itself alone in the soul; not only is its object of the natural order, but to all intents and purposes it demands that its subject as such be cut off from all supernatural life, cut off from itself as Christian. Hence is explained the absurd myth from which we are still suffering, of a man presumably in the state of pure nature in order to philosophize, who crowns himself with grace in order to merit heaven. The crown will not be long in falling away like a useless accessory. The man of nature—of fallen nature—will remain. The Cartesian revolution has been a process of secularization of wisdom.

As evidence for Descartes is a quality of our ideas—ideas which constitute science only if they are purely and absolutely luminous, and which we should sort out in order to discard everything that is obscure—a total antinomy exists henceforth between intellection and mystery. On one hand, the pure geometrical light and the pure light of the *cogito;* on the other, an impenetrable darkness. From the world of matter, which is beneath thought, thought must drive out absolutely all obscurity. Above it, it must acknowledge the obscurity of things divine; but woe to it if it tries to venture there.

Let us briefly characterize these two series of consequences of the Cartesian position.

*

* *

On the side of what is superior to man, Descartes was too intelligent to deny mystery. He deepened it rather; he made everything, even science itself, appendant to God and to His incomprehensibility, the sovereign guarantee of the value of understanding and of clear ideas.

But what remains, and what is essential to the whole future of thought, is that a *science* of mystery is henceforth impossible.

We know that in matters of religion Descartes was a fideist; he was, as he said, of the religion of his king and of his foster-mother. This fideism was accompanied by a violent antitheologism. In short, Descartes denied the possibility of *theology* as science; the only science, the only wisdom, was it not natural wisdom—philosophy? A century and a half later Kant, as though to punish that pride, will deny in his turn the possibility of *meta-physics* as science. Contempt for theology, that is, for the most exalted use that man can make of speculative reason, in familiarizing it with things pertaining to deity—contempt for theology was the first resignation, and the first betrayal, of Christian intelligence.

Concerning metaphysics itself, Descartes left an insoluble contradiction as a legacy to modern thought. On the one hand, in order that the knowledge of the existence of God may be the most certain of all knowledge, the idea of God must be a clear idea in the Cartesian system, the clearest and most distinct idea of all—an intellectual intuition. Here we have modern thought launched in the direction of ontology and of pantheism. On the other hand, the infinite is in no way intelligible to us; it is vain to speculate upon it; no science of it is possible. And there we have modern thought launched toward agnosticism. Pantheism, agnosticism, it will ceaselessly swing back and forth between the two terms of this contradiction.

To tell the truth, Descartes did not trouble himself much over the speculative conciliation of such a contradiction, as he constantly broke up the harmonies of *philosophia perennis* into two antinomic errors, each one disguising the other. He needs God as the guarantor of science; therefore he betakes himself to Him by the quickest route, one which most resembles an intuition: to know that He exists and that He guarantees the human order. Reassured of it as a practical man, he loses interest in God; it is the world which interests him now. He turns aside religiously from God. Too exalted a God! Too sublime. Let us pay our respects to the Creator with despatch. And now, bring on the world. If reason were to linger over things divine, it could only be in order to submit them to itself, since to know, for Cartesian reasoning, is to subjugate the object. A sacred flight precipitates it toward things below.

And this is what matters to us: the overturning of the intellectual order, the inversion of the impulse of knowledge, for which Descartes is doubtless not the first one responsible, but as it were the prince and legislator. Metaphysics is reduced to a justification of science; it has as its aim to make physics possible.

Aristotle said that there is more joy in knowing divine things imperfectly and obscurely than in knowing perfectly the things proportioned to our minds. And thus the nature of our intellect is to drag itself along toward divine things. Descartes on the contrary, boasted of devoting only a very few hours a year to metaphysical thoughts. In his eyes, it is important "to have thoroughly understood once in one's life the principles of metaphysics," but "it would be very harmful to occupy one's understanding in meditating upon them, because it would then be unable to attend to the functions of the imagination and the senses as well." Cartesian understanding does not drag itself along toward things divine, it settles comfortably in worldly things. Cartesian science is by essence a rich man's, a propertied man's science. What is, first of all, important to him is not the dignity of the object, even though it be obtained only through certainly not luxurious means—what is important to him is the perfection of the means, it is the comfort of clear ideas.

*

* *

With regard to what is inferior to man, to the world of corporeal nature, Cartesian intellect claims to understand everything exposed to the core, through the substance, through the essence itself. Matter lies naked before it as before the angels. The mathematical knowledge of nature, for Descartes, is not what it is in reality, a certain interpretation of phenomena, invaluable moreover, but which does not answer questions bearing upon the first principles of things. This knowledge is, for him, the revelation of the very essence of things. These are analyzed exhaustively by geometric extension and local movement. The whole of physics, that is, the whole of the philosophy of nature, is nothing but geometry.

Thus Cartesian evidence goes straight to mechanicism. It mechanizes nature, it does violence to it; it annihilates everything which causes things to symbolize with the spirit, to partake of the genius of the Creator, to speak to us. The universe becomes dumb.

And why all this? What is the end of all our effort to know?

THE DREAM OF DESCARTES

It is a practical end: to become, as Descartes puts it in the *Discourse on Method, masters and possessors of nature.* To desire to dominate and utilize material nature is a good thing! But once the direction of knowledge was reversed, as I remarked a while back, this practical domination of created force was to become two centuries after Descartes, the final aim of civilization—and that is a very great evil.

*

*   *

The cultural significance of rationalism thus becomes clearly apparent to us. It implies an anthropocentric naturalism of wisdom; and what optimism! It is a doctrine of necessary progress, of salvation by science and by reason; I mean, temporal and worldly salvation of humanity by reason alone, which, thanks to the principles of Descartes, will lead man to felicity, to "that highest degree of wisdom in which the sovereign good of human life consists" (he wrote it himself in the preface to the French translation of the *Principles*)—in giving man full mastery over nature and over his nature; and, as the Hegelians were to add two centuries later, over his history. As if reason by itself alone was capable of making men act reasonably and of securing the good of peoples! There is no worse delusion.

On the balance-sheet we should inscribe: rupture of the impulse which was directing all the labor of human science towards the eternal, toward conversation with the three divine Persons—upsetting of the élan of knowledge. Knowledge does not aspire to do more than give man the means of domesticating matter. The sole retreat remaining for the spiritual will be science's reflection upon itself. And doubtless, that is indeed something of spiritual but of an autophagous spiritual. To delude oneself with the thought that the idealistic ruminating of physics and mathematics is enough to force the gates to the kingdom of God, to introduce man to wisdom and to freedom, to transform him into a fire of love burning for all eternity, is psychological childishness and metaphysical humbug. Man becomes spiritualized only by joining with a spiritual and eternal living One. There is only one spiritual life which does not mislead—that which the Holy Spirit bestows. Rationalism is the death of spirituality.

Then it is through the experience of sin, of suffering and despair that in the nineteenth century we will see spirituality reawaken in the wilderness: through a Baudelaire, a Rimbaud. An ambiguous spirituality, good for heaven if grace takes hold of it, good for hell if pride interferes. Many of our contemporaries will seek nourishment for their souls in anti-reason, and below reason, nourishment which should be sought only above reason. And to have led so many reasoning animals around to a hatred of reason is another of rationalism's misdeeds.

*

*   *

It remains for us to consider rapidly a third aspect of Descartes' doctrine—the one which concerns human nature.

Cartesian dualism breaks man up into two complete substances, joined to one another no one knows how: on the one hand, the body which is only geometric extension; on the other, the soul which is only thought—an angel inhabiting a machine and directing it by means of the pineal gland.

I shall not emphasize here the inextricable difficulties into which Descartes has thus thrown metaphysics and psychology. The soul being only consciousness, the whole unconscious will be henceforth purely corporeal, for an unconscious phychological functioning is a contradiction in terms. On the other hand, the conflict between determinism and freedom becomes insoluble. Finally, the interaction of the body and the soul being rendered from then on unintelligible, one must have recourse to the great metaphysical myths of occasionalism, or of pre-established harmony, or of Spinozistic parallelism. An extremist spiritualism, regarding every psychic function as purely spiritual, will precipitate into materialism such sciences as medicine and neurology, which must indeed recognize that the psyche undergoes the consequential effects of body conditions. It is the Cartesian hyperspiritualism which has caused the mass-production of innumerable materialistic physicians rampant in science up to the close of the last century.

But enough of this. What I wanted to indicate was the cultural significance of Cartesian dualism, thought side, and body side.

Thought side. We know the effects of the triumph of this dualism in the second half of the seventeenth century: a theoretical contempt of the body and the senses; nothing worthwhile but pure thought. That means, in fact, the triumph of artificial thought and of false intellectualism; for human intellection is living and fresh only when it is centered upon the vigilance of sense perception. The natural roots of our knowledge being cut, a general drying-up in philosophy and culture resulted, a drought for which romantic tears were later to provide only an insufficient remedy.

In the second place, a complete disregard of the affective

life. Feeling is no longer anything more than a confused idea. The existence of love and of will as forming a distinct world, having its own life and its own laws in the heaven of the soul, is radically misunderstood. Affectivity will have its revenge. Take for example the present tendencies of psychology, which would submerge everything under affectivism and instinctivism.

In the third place, for Cartesian civilization, man is only thought. "I, that is to say, my thought," said the philosopher. Man has lost his body. Alas! The body has not, let go of him. Only the ascetics have the means of scorning the body. The Cartesian contempt for the body is a theorist's illusion. In the end, Freud will turn up with his great sadistic lyricism and claim to reduce man to sexuality and the instinct of death.

Body side. I was saying that the Cartesian man had lost his body: he has delivered it over to the universal mechanism, to the energies of matter regarded as forming a closed world. What have been the results?

First of all, man's body ceases to be regarded as human by essence. Cartesian physicians, iatromechanists or iatrochemists, treat it as an automaton or as a retort. And, in a general way, medicine tends to forget that it is dealing with a being whose life is not only corporeal, but moral and spiritual as well.

This observation ought to be generalized: we leave Descartes himself then, but not the Cartesian spirit. Let us say that in the modern world, everything which is amenable to any technique whatever in human life tends to resolve itself into a closed world, separate, independent. Things like politics and economics in particular will become contrivances removed from the specific regulation of the human good; they will cease to be, as the ancients wished, subordinated intrinsically and of themselves, to ethics.

With greater reason, speculative science and art, which do not appertain of themselves to the domain of ethics, will impose on man a law which is not his own.

Here is man then, the centre of the world, of a world inhuman in every respect, pressing in upon him. Nothing in human life is any longer made to man's measure, to the rhythm of the human heart. The forces he has unleashed, split him asunder.

He wishes to reign nevertheless, and more than ever—and over his own nature. But how? By technique alone—that is, by means extraneous to himself. Thus we arrive at the great dispute of our age, freedom by technique versus freedom by self-determination.

I should like to put it in this way: there are two ways of looking at man's mastery of himself. Man can become master of his nature by imposing the law of reason—of reason aided by grace—on the universe of his own inner energies. That work, which in itself is a construction in love, requires that our branches be pruned to bear fruit: a process called *mortification*. Such a morality is an ascetic morality.

What rationalism claims to impose upon us today is an entirely different morality, anti-ascetic, exclusively technological. An appropriate technique should permit us to rationalize human life, *i.e.*, to satisfy our desires with the least possible inconvenience, without any interior reform of ourselves. What such a morality subjects to reason are material forces and agents exterior to man, instruments of human life; it is not man, nor human life as such. It does not free man, it weakens him, it disarms him, it renders him a slave to all the atoms of the universe, and especially to his own misery and egoism. What remains of man? A consumer crowned by science. This is the final gift, the twentieth century gift of the Cartesian reform.

Technique is good—mechanics is good. I disapprove of the spirit of archaism which would suppress the machine and technique. But if mechanics and technique are not mastered, subjected by force to the good of man, that is to say entirely and rigorously subordinated to religious ethics and made instruments of an ascetic morality, humanity is literally lost.

*

* *

How then shall we characterize the cultural significance of Cartesian dualism? To sum up the preceding observations, let us say that this dualism carries along with it both an anthropocentric angelism and materialism of civilization. On the balance-sheet must be written: division of man, rupture of the human life. They began by putting the human self above everything else, an angelic self—nay, a divine self. It is so perfectly one that no plurality of powers or of faculties is to be distinguished in it! Its substance is the very act of thinking.

This Cartesian man, naturally good in so far as he is reason, will later become the man of Rousseau, naturally good in so far as he is sentiment and instinct, and whom social life and reflection corrupt. He has no further need to perfect himself, to build himself up by his virtues, he has only to blossom forth, to display himself by virtue of sincerity. It is as though one were to tell a fertilized egg to be sincere and not to have the hypocrisy to construct its form by its own efforts, through a host of morphogenetic choices and differentiations which cruelly limit its availability.

Reflection has progressed prodigiously. Never has man more

carefully scrutinized his innermost recesses. Never has he experienced so heart-rending a nostalgia for freedom. Yet how is he truly to know freedom? His own personality escapes him, he is a prey to that duality characterized so well by Nicolas Berdiaev in the most thoughtful pages of his book on Dostoievsky.

IV

The misfortune of our classical age is to have been as though caught fast in the conflict between two geniuses, one of which was making of man an angel full of clear ideas—the other a monster of darkness. If we had to choose between Descartes and Pascal, it is obviously Pascal's part that we would take. I cannot believe that the Cartesians of our day who hate Pascal do so through mental incompetence, but rather that they stop up their ears in order not to hear him. For that matter, Descartes himself would have repudiated them, since no object to which the mind can adhere remains for them, no everlasting element, nothing but empty mechanisms and forms without content. What worse confession of impotence for Cartesian reason, than to acknowledge, as a great French poet seems sometimes to do when he philosophizes on his art, nothing more than pure vacuity, and an exercise of self-awareness and word fabrication working out only nothingness?

The fact remains that Pascal, knocking his saintly and generous heart against the narrow precincts of the Jansenist system, also failed (as did Descartes in a contrary sense) to understand nature and reason.

Are we going to waver endlessly between Descartes and Pascal? It is not between Descartes and Pascal that we must choose; the problem thus posed is without a solution. St. Thomas Aquinas is the one who answers the errors of Descartes without getting rid of anything true that Descartes has grasped.

I hope no one will misunderstand my criticism of Descartes. In the first place, I am perfectly well aware that Descartes is neither the only one, nor the first one responsible for the morbid elements which encumber our philosophical heredity. These morbid elements were fermenting well before his time. But he gave them a form, a countenance—all the energy which comes from a powerful systematization.

And then, what I have criticized is less Descartes than the Cartesian spirit. I mean, that which the ideas set down by Descartes in modern thought, in virtue of their internal logic, and taking into account historical contingencies, would necessarily engender of themselves.

Finally, I am not forgetting what I pointed out at the beginning: namely, that it is is not a question of destroying all that Descartes has left us; that would be simply absurd. Not only did he bring about considerable progress in the physical and mathematical sciences; not only did he keep many of the ancient treasures—many more than his offspring have kept; not only did he himself have great intuitions, but what is more, certain developments of primary importance demanded by historical growth of thought were stimulated by his errors: physico-mathematical science was founded, and reflexivity carved out its own domain in philosophy . . .

Having made these qualifications, I can point out the gravity of the three great ruptures noted above: the rupture of thought with being, of the movement of the soul toward wisdom, and of the human compound.

THE DREAM OF DESCARTES

I believe that Russian philosophy is fond of setting off the *theandric* conception which recognizes that the Word was made flesh and views everything in the light of the Incarnation, against the *anthropotheistic* conception which insists that man be made god, and which ordinates everything to this conquest of divinity. It is quite true that human affairs in actual fact necessarily follow along the line of one or the other of these two conceptions. Well! Descartes gave anthropotheism its philosophical letters of credit. That is why we make war on him.

I have often said that Descartes (or Cartesianism) has been the great French sin in modern history. It is as though searching our own souls that we Frenchmen should, in my opinion, conduct an examination of the Cartesian reform. I think that this is the only suitable method for bringing about a reconciliation of minds in truth, in particular a mutual understanding between the East and the West. Perhaps it would be advantageous for Russian philosophy to do for Hegel—as well as for English and American philosophy to do for John Locke—what I have tried to do for Descartes. In any case, I beg the good reader to believe that if Cartesianism has been the French sin in modern history, things other than this sin have been at work in French thought.

NOTES

NOTES

1. *"Tu enim revera solus es, qui desidiosum excitasti, jam e memoria pene elapsam eruditionem revocasti, et a seriis occupationibus aberrans ingenium ad meliora reduxisti"* (23rd of April, 1619, A.T., vol. X, p. 162-163).

As Gustave Cohen has already pointed out, the date of the discovery of the admirable Science, November 10, 1619, was the anniversary of Descartes' first visit to Beeckman.

2. " . . . He so fatigued himself that his brain became fired, and he fell into a sort of rapture which had such an effect on his already-downcast spirit, that it was in a state to receive impressions of dreams and visions." BAILLET, *Vie de monsieur des Cartes*, A.T., X, p. 181.

3. *Olympica*, a manuscript now lost; Leibnitz copied several passages from it in 1675-1676, upsing the Clerselier papers, and Baillet has summarized it in his *Vie de monsieur des Cartes* (1691), quoting the first lines of it.

The following year on almost the same date, the philosopher made another discovery. In a marginal note to the passage we are quoting here, and in a later handwriting, is found the following remark, according to Baillet's account: *XI Novembris 1620, coepi intelligere fundamentum inventi mirabilis*. According to the work devoted to this second discovery by G. Milhaud (*Revue de métaphysique et de morale*, March-April 1918), the *admirable invention* in question was that of the refracting telescope, an invention made quite by chance in the first few years of the XVII century, by Jacques Metius, the mathematical basis of which was perceived by Descartes in 1620.

4. G. Milhaud has clearly shown (*Revue de métaphysque et de morale*, July 1916, pp. 610-611) that the interpretation according to which the discovery of the admirable Science had taken place *during the day* of November 10, 1619, and would thus have preceded the paroxysm of rapture marked by the dream (*during the night* of the 10th-11th) is due simply to Baillet's imagination and to the freedom with which he translates the Latin text of the philosopher. A careful study of Descartes' "mystical seizure" forces Milhaud to conclude that on the contrary, the plenitude of enthusiasm, the dream and the discovery are but one and the same event.

5. Maxime Leroy, who rightly points out that this dream proclaims a state not only of intellectual but moral crisis, had the idea of questioning the author of the *Traumdeutung* on the subject. The answer

189

given by Freud, who himself draws attention to the unreliability of interpretations made when there is no possibility of questioning the sleeper, contains nothing particularly significant, unless it be a quite gratuitous interpretation of the melon, and the remark that Descartes' dream belongs in a category of dreams (Träume von Oben) whose content is very close to the conscious thought and preoccupations of the waking state.

6. This phrase is quoted in a marginal note by Baillet, as an extract from the *Olympica*.

"That is why," writes Baillet, "God did not allow him to advance further, and to let himself be carried off, even to a holy place, by a Spirit which He had not sent; although he was quite persuaded that it had been the Spirit of God which had made him take the first steps toward that church. The terror with which he was struck in the second dream marked, as he thought, his synderesis, that is to say, his remorse for the sins he might have committed during the course of his life up to that moment." A.T., X, p. 186.

7. " . . . He then addressed himself to the Holy Virgin," says Baillet, "to commend to her that thing *which he judged the most important of his life;* and in order more urgently to interest this Blessèd Mother of God, he took the occasion of a journey he was thinking of making to Italy in a few days, to make the vow of a pilgrimage to Notre-Dame-de-Lorette." A.T., *ibid.*

8. Maxime Leroy casts doubt upon the reality of the pilgrimage. It is in fact possible that Baillet stated that it took place on the occasion of the journey of 1624, basing his statement only on the promise that Descartes had made and on the opportunity offered by the philosopher's stay in Venice. Leroy goes too far however when he states elsewhere as an established fact, that Descartes "did not go on a pilgrimage to Notre-Dame-de-Lorette" (*Descartes, le philosophe au maque,* vol. I, p. 93). What one can say without fear of being mistaken is that Leroy's wish that his hero should have forgotten his vow is as strong as in Baillet the wish that he should have fulfilled it, in the midst of "most edifying" circumstances. Besides, Leroy must have been quite aware of the fact that even if Descartes had fulfilled his vow he would not have gone "to adore" the Virgin of Lorette.

9. Louis Dimier is content to remark modestly: "All those who, gifted with some degree of imagination, have known at the age of twenty those fevers and ardors of a thought which is seeking itself, which finds itself and leaps forth, recapture as they read this episode in Baillet, touching and delightful memories." (*Descartes*, p. 23.)

10. Baillet here relies upon a text of a manuscript now lost (*Studium bonae mentis*), as his only authority, which he amplifies according to his custom, and in which Descartes averred he had not been able to discover anything certain on the subject of the Rosicrucians, *necdum de illis*

NOTES

quidquam certi compertum habeo. But can one ever know anything certain about an occult society? Father Poisson, just as devoted to Descartes' cause as Baillet, writes for his part: "He knew them nevertheless, *either by reputation* OR OTHERWISE, and was perfectly right in saying that they were nothing but foolish people." (*Rem. sur la méth. de René Descartes*, Vendôme, 1670, Part II, 1st Observation, quoted in A.T., X, 197a). One can further remark with Charles Adam that among the notes taken by Leibnitz from the juvenilia of Descartes is found the mention of a *Polybii Cosmopolitani Thesaurus mathematicus,* a work either written or more possibly remaining in the project stage, that Descartes dedicated to "the scholars of the entire world, and especially to the Rosicrucian brotherhood, very famous in Germany, *totius orbis eruditis et specialiter celeberrimis in G. (Germania) F.R.C."* (cf. A.T., X, p. 214).

Maxime Leroy, in his chapter on *Les Heures rosi-cruciennes* (*op. cit.,* vol. I, pp. 68 ff.) comes out very definitely for the hypothesis according to which the young Descartes must have been profoundly influenced by the Rosicrucians. He provides several indications which confirm to a remarkable degree those that I give here.

11. See the study published by G. MILHAUD in *Scientia,* February number, 1918.

12. An eminent mathematician, Faulhaber linked up his mathematical studies with speculations on the mystic of numbers mentioned in the Book of Daniel and in the Apocalypse. It was by the apocalyptic number 666 that he had been led to discover a stereometric analogue to the theorem of Pythagoras—Cf. HOCHSSTETTER in *Algemeine deutsche Biographie;* WEYERMANN, *Nachrichten von Gelehrten. Künstlern aus Ulm,* Ulm, 1798.

13. The "link between the knowledge of self and the knowledge of God, which is its foundation, and the mode of expression of this intuition" cannot—so Jacques Chevalier thinks (Descartes, 1925, p. 47)—be identified with the admirable science. As Descartes himself indicates at the beginning of Part IV of the *Discourse,* these are the fruits of the "first meditations" that he made after having retired to Holland at the end of 1628. Everything shows moreover that the discovery of 1619 was not so formally philosophical in character; and on the other hand, the expression *scientia mirabilis* was not suitable for designating the victory over doubt by means of the *cogito* and its linking up with the existence of God. These things are contained in the intuition of the admirable science in a potential manner only.

14. "But after I had thus spent several years studying in the book of the world, and trying to acquire some experience, I resolved one day to study within myself, as well . . ." *Disc. de la Méth.,* Part I, A.T., VI, p. 10.

15. *The Discours de la Méthode,* as we know, was only a preface to

a scientific treatise which was to contain "some test-examples of that Method" (Refraction, Meteors and Geometry). The title Descartes first thought of using was as follows: *Project of a universal Science capable of raising our nature to its highest degree of perfection. To which is added Refraction, Meteors and Geometry, in which the most curious matters the author could choose in order to provide proof of the universal science which he is proposing, are treated in such a way that even those who have not studied can understand them.*

16. *Discours de la Méthode,* part II, A.T., VI, p. 12.

"*Scientia est velut mulier; quae, si pudica apud virum maneat, colitur; si communis fiat, vilescit,*" he wrote in 1619 (*Cogitationes privatae,* collected by Leibnitz, A.T., X, p. 214.

17. Preface to the French translation of the *Principia philosophiae,* A.T., IX, part II, p. 8.

18. *Ibid.,* p. 9.

19. *Discours de la Méthode,* part VI, A.T., VI, p. 62.

20. *Sapientia,* VII, 8.

21. "I know too that several centuries may go by before all the truths it is possible to deduce from these principles have been deduced." (*Principes,* preface to the French translation, A.T., IX, part II, p. 20.)

22. *Discours de la Méthode,* part II, A.T., VI, p. 15.

23. For the ancients, it is only by acquiring such a quality (the *habitus* of a science) that human reason adapts itself to the object of that science. Descartes declares on the contrary: "Since the principles are clear, and since one must deduce nothing from them except by very evident reasoning, *one always has enough wit to understand things which depend upon them.*" (Preface to the French translation of the *Principia,* A.T., LX, part II, p. 15.)

24. "Mirum videri possit, quare graves sententiae in scriptis poetarum, magis quam philosophorum. Ratio est quod poetae per enthusiasmum et vim imaginationis scripsere: sunt in nobis semina scientiae, ut in silice, quae per rationem a philosophis educuntur, per imaginationem a poetis excutiuntur magisque elucent." (*Cogitationes privatae,* collected by Leibnitz, A.T., X, p. 217.)

25. The symbols of the Dictionary and the *Corpus Poetarum* are invaluable for the historian. They show that as early as 1619 Descartes had conceived the central idea of the unity of the sciences, of which he was to give a philosophically elaborated theory in the *Regulae* of 1628. He wrote furthermore, in 1619, what was already a very clear expression of that idea: "*Larvatae nunc scientiae sunt: quae, larvis sublatis, pulcherrimae apparerent. Catenam scientiarum videnti, non difficilius videbitur, eas animo retinere, quam seriem numerorum.*" (*Cogitationes privatae,* A.T., X, p. 215.) It will be for the *masked philosopher* (see below, note 37) to unmask the sciences and to make their continuity and their unity appear with their beauty.

NOTES

26. In the application and when he reaches the physical sciences, Descartes will be forced to make a place for experience. But if the rôle of experience was considerable *in fact* in the scientific activity of Descartes himself—*by right* and in the Cartesian theory, science was to remain a pure deductive construction starting from innate ideas, claiming to proceed always from cause to effect, and as a result, excluding strictly inductive procedure. Experience, which thus remains extrinsic to science, has as its sole function that of propounding questions to the philosopher, and of selecting from among several equally possible *deductions* those which correspond to the world actually posed in existence by God.

27 "It was the eve of St. Martin, when it was the custom in the place where he was then staying, to indulge in revelry as was the case in France. But he assures us that he had passed the evening and the whole day in great sobriety, and that for three whole months he had not drunk a drop of wine." BAILLET, A.T., X, p. 186.

28. Hamelin, like Bordas-Demoulin, has been quite right in sensing this about the Cartesian doctrine of eternal truths. If in the last analysis these truths depend, as Descartes insists, not on divine essence itself as the eternal object of divine intellection, but on creative liberty— in such a way that God might have been able to make possible a square circle or a mountain without a vallel—our knowledge of these truths no longer derives its certainty from the fact that it rests on the necessity of ideal essences, but rather that it results from a natural revelation instructing us in what, effectively, divine liberty has chosen. "As our innate ideas come from God, it is certain that they represent the truths God has established. But on the other hand, as God is incomprehensible, we cannot hope to attain the core of His essence and we see only what He allows us to see. Human knowledge, instead of embracing veritable necessities, deals only with necessities *for us*—that is to say, not with necessities but with facts; and however natural that revelation may be, the person was not wrong who said (Bordas-Demoulin) that our knowledge, from this point of view, is only a revelation." (O. HAMELIN, *Le Système de Descartes*, p. 233.)

If one turns to the Cartesian theory of evidence, one still arrives at the same conclusion. This theory is copied directly from the theological doctrine of faith. What we conceive clearly and distinctly is infallibly true *because it is guaranteed by divine veracity*, exactly as the articles of faith are infallibly true because they are guaranteed by the authority of revealing God. From Descartes' pen, when he happens to recall in his way the common teaching on the certitude of faith, one finds again the same terms he uses with regard to the certitude of evidence: ". . . we have an absolutely certain confidence that the things which are proposed for us to believe were revealed by Him, *and that it is quite impossible for Him to be guilty of falsehood and to deceive us.*" (Rép. aux IIes objections, A.T., IX, part I, p. 116.)

29. See p. 60-61, and note 58.

30. Theology is also a universal science (at once and preëminently speculative and practical), as is metaphysics to a lesser degree and in the exclusively speculative order. But unlike the unique science of Descartes, metaphysical wisdom and the superior wisdom of theology do not suppress to their own advantage and absorb into themselves the other sciences and their specific diversity.

31. Confirmation of these views will be found in the important work published since that time by ETIENNE GILSON, *Etudes sur le rôle de la Pensée Médiévale dans la formation du système cartésien*, Paris, Vrin, 1930.

32. This urgency, from the standpoint of the interests of Christian spiritualism, appears all the greater since the knowledge of the physical world is to change in character, and to be orientated exclusively toward the mathematical study of well-established appearances, that is to say, toward phenomena. Now, according to the profound remark of Pierre Termier (*Le témoignage des sciences*, in *La Joie de connaître*, p. 322), physical appearances, the image of the boundless world of Galileo and Descartes—like the image of the Aristotelian spheres—in short *"phenomena do not seem very Christian."* This is not surprising, for nature is Christian only in its moaning, and tells of the glory of God only to those who understand more than the noise made by appearances. Nevertheless, as most men judge according to their senses and imagination, the imagery of a science which was to be absorbed by phenomena ran grave risk of shifting the intellectual notion that Christianity has of the world. Hence the necessity of returning *ad intus*, of retempering the vigor of the metaphysical intellect by applying it with greater force to the things of the human, moral and spiritual order. There, undoubtedly, lay the providential mission of a Descartes.

33. As Gilson points out (*La Liberté chez Descartes et la Théologie*, Paris, 1913, p. 437, cf. pp. 94-95), while he cloaks himself in religion in order to gain the approval of the Sorbonne, Descartes writes to Mersenne that it is a question of achieving a success for his physics (January 28, 1641, A.T., III, 297-298: "And I must say, between ourselves, that these six Meditations contain the whole foundation of my Physics. But please do not mention that; for if you did, those who favor Aristotle would perhaps raise more difficulty in approving them; and I hope that those who read them will little by little become accustomed to my principles and will recognize their truth before perceiving that they destroy those of Aristotle.")

With regard to the respective importance of physics and of metaphysics in Descartes' thought, the *Etudes sur le rôle de la pensée médiévale dans la formation du système cartésien*, published in 1930 by

NOTES

ETIENNE GILSON (pp. 174-184) provide a more flexible and more care-fully-shaded interpretation than the one given in his earlier work.

34. The pagan philosopher, especially the Platonist and the Gnostic, had a similar movement (*after*, however, he had reached the peak of rational knowledge), but because he demanded of philosophy an inferior analogical equivalent of that which the Christian possesses through the theological virtues and the gifts of the Holy Ghost.

35. When we speak of Cartesian idealism as "shutting thought up within itself," it is perfectly clear that we do not mean to attribute to Descartes the doctrine of Berkeley or Kant; neither do we claim that Des-cartes denied either the reality of the exterior world or the existence of real objects known by means of our ideas. We do not mean that for him the only object reached *directly and immediately* by the act of knowing is thought—not things. And thus although his intentions may have been realist, in actual fact he has propounded the *problem* and introduced the *principle* of modern idealism.

BOUTROUX stated it very well: "The main problem of Cartesian meta-physics is the passing from thought to existence. Thought alone is indissolubly inherent in itself. How then, by what right and in what sense can we affirm existences? . . . Existence for the ancients was a thing given and perceived which one had only to analyze; in the present case it is a distant object which must be attained, if indeed it is possible to do so . . ." (*Revue de Métaphysique et de Morale*, May 1894.)

36. *A propos de la révolution cartésienne, Physique mathématique et Philosophie scolastique*, Revue Thomiste, April-June 1918. An article reproduced in *Réflexions sur l'Intelligence*, chap. VI.

37. 1619, calendis Januarii. "Ut comoedi, moniti ne in fronte appareat pudor, personam induunt; sic ego, hoc mundi theatrum conscensurus, in quo hactenus spectator existiti, larvatus prodeo." *Cogitationes privatae* (texts collected by Leibnitz), A.T., X, 213.

This *larvatus prodeo*, upon which I myself have rather insisted, both in the present work (*Les Lettres*, Feb. 1922), and in *Trois Réformateurs* (Paris, Plon, 1925) furnished the subject for a book by Maxime Leroy (*Descartes, le philosophe au masque*, Paris, Rieder, 1929). Leroy either did not read my studies or considered them as non-existent, since he made no allusion whatsoever to them. I explained in *Trois Réformateurs* (note 32 of the first editions, 52 of the 14th) why I thought that the sentence in question had been written by Descartes not before, but after the dream of November 10th, 1619.

38. G. MILHAUD, *Descartes savant*, Paris, 1921.

39. A.T., I, 194 (to Mersenne, December 23, 1630). — Concerning the theory of the eternal truths freely willed by God, Leibnitz (who was an expert in intellectual diplomacy) said somewhat spitefully: "It was apparently one of his tricks, one of his philosophical ruses; he was preparing some loop-hole, just as he found an expedient for denying

the movement of the earth when all the time he was an out-and-out Copernican." (*Théodicée*, II, §186.)

40. To M. Pastel, March 24, 1701.

41. MAURICE BLONDEL, *Le Christianisme de Descartes*, Revue de Métaph. et de Morale, 1896.

42. A.T., I, 137 (to Mersenne, April 15, 1630).

43. A.T., I, 370 (to XXX, April 27, 1637?).

44. A.T., VII, 603 (Letter to Father Dinet).

45. A.T., III, 492 (January 1642). Translation.

46. *Principes*, III, 19 (A.T., IX, 2nd part, 109): "That I deny the movement of the earth with greater care than Copernicus, and greater truth than Tycho."

47. BAILLET, II, p. 88.—Cf. letters to Mersenne, A.T., III, 185, 251, 481, 470. "I assure you," the philosopher writes in the last of these (December 22, 1641), "that if I have any interest in being in their good graces, they have perhaps no less interest in being in mine, and in not being opposed to my plans: for, if they were they would force me to examine some one of their Manuals, and to examine it in such a way as to bring unending shame upon them."

48. To Father Charlet, A.T., IV, 157; February 9, 1645.—"For having undertaken to write a philosophy," he writes to Father Dinet, "I know that your Order alone can do more than anything else in the world to make it or break it." (Same date, A.T., IV. 159.)

49. To Father Charlet, A.T., IV, 157.

50. To the same; A.T., IV, 141; October 1644.

51. E. GILSON, *La Liberté chez Descartes et la théologie*, Paris, 1913, p. 441.

52. *De l'action de Dieu sur les créatures*, 2 vol., Paris, 1714.

53. Cf. *Principes*, III, 47 (A.T., IX, part 2, 125-126): "The laws of nature [are] such that even though we were to imagine the chaos of the poets, that is, a complete confusion of all parts of the universe, we could always prove that by means of these laws that confusion must return little by little to the order now present in the world, [. . .] these laws being cause that matter successively takes on all the forms of which it is capable."

54. Here we have a curious example of the way in which Cartesian thought causes a traditional doctrine to *lapse into materiality*. The distortion of the Scholastic doctrine of the conservation of things by God,—a distortion more evident in Descartes' followers than in himself, but which he nevertheless started—comes from the notion of time as composed of separate instants. Cf. O. HAMELIN, *le Système de Descartes*, p. 223; JEAN WAHL, *Du rôle de l'idée de l'instant dans la philosophie de Descartes*, Paris, 1920. See also chapter IV of the present work, pp. 180-182.

55. E. GILSON, *La Liberté chez Descartes et la théologie*, p. 441.

NOTES

56. "If then one wishes seriously to seek the truth, one must not apply oneself to a single science; they are all linked up with one another and are interdependent." *Reg.* I, A.T., X, 361 (trans.). That is what the ancients taught concerning moral virtues (connected because they depend, all of them, upon prudence, which in turn depends upon them). Cf. *Sum. Theol.*, I-II, 65, 1.

On the contrary (*Ibid.*, ad 3) the intellectual virtues and the sciences are not connected with each other, for if they depend upon the intelligence of the principles, the reverse is not true; each one then pursues its own particular way.

57. "Credendumque est, ita omnes inter se esse connexas, ut longe facilius sit cunctas simul addiscere, quam unicam ab aliis separare." *Reg.* I, p. 361. In order to retain the element of truth contained in this affirmation, let us note that in the Scholastic conception it would apply, at least by right, to all the sciences which constitute a single *order* of knowledge, for example, to all the mathematical sciences: specialization here is only a servitude imposed upon the human mind with respect to its weakness (while between the mathematician and the naturalist for example, it is imposed with respect to the object).

58. If the theory of the unity of science was described at great length in the *Regulae* of 1628, and if one sentence of the first rule (the one cited on p. 61, and note 57) seems to be copied in the *Disputationes metaphysicae* by Suarez, disp. XLIV *de Habitibus*, sect. 11, n. 59 (where it expresses not the author's thought but an adversary's) it is nevertheless as early as 1619 that Descartes became conscious, in a flash of intuition, of the significance and importance of that idea. See above, note 25.

For us, who have not the same reasons as Descartes for regarding the dream of November 10, 1619, as a supernatural revelation, and who consider it a dream (*Traum von Oben*, Freud calls it) where the preoccupations and the meditations of the waking state played a large part, there is no ground either for supposing that the idea of the unity of science could have sprung up all of a sudden in the mind of the philosopher that night. The way was prepared for it by a series of reflections, in which Descartes' reading could and must have played its part. SIRVEN, in his thesis on *Les Années d'apprentissage de Descartes* (Albi, 1928), points out that Antoine de Bernardis (1503-1565) had already upheld that idea, which had been contested by Fonseca, the Coimbrians and Suarez.

But for these Scholastics, it was merely a question of a new (and incorrect) opinion on the connection between the sciences—more perfectly acquired, according to the opinion under discussion, if they pertain to a single *habitus* developed in the mind; in any case, the sciences continued to pertain to a *habitus*, and to be conceived on the traditional pattern. With Descartes, it is altogether different. For him the idea of the unity of science has an incomparably deeper meaning. On the one hand, it is linked up in his mind with the negation of the qualities and the *habitus;* if science is one, of the very unity of Thought, that is because it is Thought itself unfurling. On the other hand, it is the possibility of a substantially new science that Descartes thus perceives; and the unity of this science extends a single type of intellection to the whole realm of knowledge—the mathematical type of intellection. "The idea of the unity of the body of sciences . . . is chronologically and logically inseparable from the extension of the mathematical method to the domain of knowledge in its totality." (GILSON, *Disc. de la Méth., texte et commentaire,* Paris, 1925, p. 214.) In the intuition of the *scientia mirabilis* (as later in the *Regulae*) there is the idea of the unity of science, but there is also much more—there are all the virtual riches related to this idea, and on which I tried to throw some light in the preceding chapter.

Whatever its sources, the fact remains that the idea of the unity of science, in the form it takes in Descartes, contains nothing less than a revolution for philosophy.

59. "Repraesentatio specierum, licet determinet intellectum ad cognitionem objecti, non tamen praebet intellectui inclinationem et determinationem ad utendum speciebus, et ordinandum illas; haec enim duo ad scientiam exiguuntur, assimilatio ad res, quae fit per speciem, et determinatio, seu virtus ad discernendum, quae fit per habitum." JOHN OF ST. THOMAS, *Curs. theol., in* III., P., q. 11, a,8, n. 16 (Vivès, t. VIII, p. 411). Cf. *Ibid. in* I-II, q. 52, disp. 13, a,5; CAJETAN, *in* I-II, q. 54, a,4.

60. JOHN OF ST. THOMAS, *Curs theol., in* I-II, q. 52, disp. 13. a. 5 (Vivès, t. VI, p. 294). According to Descartes on the contrary, we know at once all we can know of each known truth. (*Reg.,* XII, A.T., X, 420.) Cf. HANNEQUIN, *La méthode de Descartes,* Rev. de Métaph. et de Morale, 1906.

61. " . . . Sentiet omnino se nihil amplius ignorare ingenii defectu, vel artis, nec quidquam prorsus ab alio homine sciri posse, cujus etiam non sit capax, modo tantum ad illud idem, ut par est, mentem applicet." (*Reg.,* VIII, A.T., X, p. 396.)

62. In fact, you will say, did Descartes not succeed in making an astronomer of the sheomaker Dirck Rembrantz?—Quite so, but it was precisely by becoming his master, and by developing a *habitus* in him. It is clear that the Cartesian idea of science being an illusion, the manner in which Descartes practiced it could not very well conform to that idea. When his mathematical *habitus* is involved he is perfectly well aware that even with the help of all the rules of the method, the common sense "naturally equal in all men" is not enough. Speaking to young Burman about the science of mathematics, "omnes autem homines," he said, "ad eam apti non sunt, sed requiritur ad id *ingenium mathematicum, quodque usu poliri debet."* A.T., V, 176.—Cf. Letter to XXX,

NOTES

August, 1638(?), A.T., II, 347: " . . . without more intelligence than the common run, one cannot hope to accomplish anything very extraordinary in regard to the human sciences."

Let us recall that if *science* in the way Descartes understands it is for everybody, such is not the case for the preliminary *doubt*. (*Méth.*, 2nd part.)

63. To Mersenne, February 9, 1639, A.T., II, 501.

64. Cf. *Regulae*, II (A.T., X, 366; trans.): "Those who seek the direct road to truth should not bother with any object of which they cannot have a certitude equal to the demonstrations of arithmetic and geometry;" III (*ibid.*, 367): "We are warned furthermore, never to mix any conjecture with our judgments on the truth of things."

65. "Quam qui habet (scientiam) non sane multum aliena desiderat, atque adeo valde proprie autarkēs appellatur," to Hogeland, February 8, 1640 (A.T., XIII, 2-3). It is a question of self-sufficiency in mathematics. But how typical such a word is, in itself!

66. Preface to the French translation of the *Principia*, A.T., IX, 2nd part, p. 20.

67. "I have never taken such good care of myself as at present," Descartes wrote to Huygens, January 25, 1638, "and whereas I used to think that death could only rob me of thirty or forty years at the most, it cannot overtake me now without robbing me of the hope of more than a hundred years." (A.T., I, 507.)

Baillet relates: "The abbé Picot was so convinced of the certainty of his knowledge on this point, that he would have sworn that it was impossible for him to die as he did at the age of fifty-four, and that had it not been for a foreign and violent cause (like the one which put his machine out of gear in Sweden) he would have lived for five hundred years, after having discovered how to live for several centuries." (BAILLET, *Vie*, II, 452.)

Desmaizeaux writes in another connection, in his *Vie de Saint-Evremond*:

"During a visit to Descartes in Holland, Sir Kenelin Digby urged him to devote himself especially to the great knowledge he had of the human body in order to discover the way to prolong its existence. M. Descartes assured him he had already meditated on that subject, and that he could not promise to make man immortal, but that he was sure he could make his life as long as the life of the patriarchs. M. de Saint-Evremond, in acquainting me with this curious detail, said that it was quite well-known in Holland and that the abbé Picot, his disciple and martyr, was so convinced of his master's proficiency in the subject that for a long time he could not believe in his death."

Descartes, however, in writing to Chanut in 1646 (he probably had not had time to *carry out all the experiments that would have been*

199

necessary to support and justify his reasoning*), says: "Instead of finding the means of preserving life, I have found another, which is easier and surer, and that is to have no fear of death." (15th of June, 1646, A.T., IV, 442.)

68. *Les Rapports de la Raison et de la Foi selon Descartes*, Revue des Jeunes, October 10, 1920. Reprinted later in *La Pensée religieuse de Descartes*, Paris, 1924.

69. Leibnitz rightly observed that Descartes "passed, by a kind of leap, to the examination of difficult questions, without having explained their ingredients." (Letter to Bossuet, Bar-le-Duc edition, XI, 284.)

70. Descartes however goes beyond the traditional teaching, it seems, in that he appears to regard the fact of revelation as being in itself the object of an *evidence* ("clarté ou évidence," A.T., 116) properly so-called, of supernatural origin. "Although they say that faith has as its object things that are obscure, nevertheless the cause of our belief [that is, the fact that they have been revealed by God] is not obscure, *but is* CLEARER *than any natural light.*" (*Ibid.*, 115.)—"Veritas prima revelans est id *quod et quo creditur*," say the theologians, and not "*id quod videtur et quo creditur.*"

On the other hand, there is in Cartesian thought—in virtue of the fact that for it, everything which is not established with *geometric or more than geometric evidence* has no value as proof—a tendency to diminish too greatly, to reduce almost to the vanishing point the rôle of rational preparation for the act of faith and the value of the proofs of natural credibility (which are of a moral, not a geometrical order). Philosophical rationalism, if it remains Christian, thus tends toward fideism in religion.

71. St. Thomas, *De Veritate*, q. 14, a. 1.

72. *Ibid.*, q. 14, a. 3, ad 8.

73. Cf. *de Veritate*, q. 14, a. 3, ad 5: "Si loqueremur de eis quantum ad id quod est cognitionis tantum, sic neque opinio neque fides esset virtus, cum non habeant completam cognitionem, sed tantummodo scientia." *Sum. theol.*, I-II, 67, 3: "Fides in sui ratione habet imperfectionem ex parte subjecti, ut scilicet credens non videat id quod credit."

When so competent a critic as M. Rousselot writes in this connection that of all the great Doctors he knows none "who *scorn* faith as knowledge as much as St. Thomas does" (*L'intellectualisme de saint Thomas*, 2nd edition, p. 194), this slightly impressionistic formula, which yields to the temptation of expressing a correct idea in an incorrect way, *sensibilizing* it in order to season it to our taste, demands a healthy interpretation.

74. Cf. St. Thomas, Sum. Theol., I, 12, 13, ad 3: "Fides cognitio

---

*Letter-preface to the French translation of the *Principia*, A.T., IX, 2nd part, 17.

NOTES

quaedam est, inquantum intellectus determinatur per fidem ad alquod cognoscibile."

75. JOHN OF ST. THOMAS, *Curs. Theol.*, in I-II, q. 110, disp. 22, a. 1 (Vivès, t. VII, p. 28-29).

76. Gardeil's Gloss (*Créd.*, 48) on *de Trin.*, 2, 2.

77. JOHN OF ST. THOMAS, *Curs. theol.*, *in* II-II, q. 1, disp. 2, a. 1 (Vivès, t. VII, p. 28-29).

78. Letter to Buitendijck (1643?) : *Fides enim ad voluntatem pertinet.* A.T., IV, 63. Descartes affirms this absolutely, while in the traditional teaching faith was said to be *in voluntate sicut in causa, in intellectu sicut in subjecto.*

Cf. in addition the *answers to the second objections:* "Distinction must be made between the subject-matter or the thing to which we give our belief, and the formal reason which moves *our will to give it . . .* The clearness or evidence by which *our will can be excited to believe . . .*" A.T., IX, 115, 116.

79. *Annales de Philosophie chrétienne*, 1911, p. 638.

80. *Spiritual Canticle, str.* 11.

81. "During this life we adhere to this substance of Faith, even though it hides itself under a silvery covering; but it will appear fully revealed in heaven, and that pure gold we shall contemplate with delight." (*Ibid.*) Cf. ST. THOMAS, *De Verit.* q. 14, a. 1, ad 8: "Lux illa spiritualis [divinitus adveniens perfecte participabitur a nobis] in patria, ubi ea quae nunc credimus, perfecte videbimus. Nunc autem quod non manifeste appareant ea ad quae lux illa cognoscenda perficit, est ex defectiva participatione ipsius, non ex efficacia ipsius spiritualis luminis."

82. ST. THOMAS, *De Veritate*, q. 14, a. 2. Cf. *Ibid.*, ad 1: "Fides est prima inchoatio et fundamentum quoddam quasi totius spiritualis vitae, sicut substantia est fundamentum omnium entium." It is the same doctrine that St. John of the Cross was to develop.

83. An exception must be made for Maxime Leroy. Some of his arguments must seem impressive, at least to a rather superficial psychology, which ignores in general the concrete complexity of such problems, and especially the state of men's minds during the time of Descartes. On the contrary, the more one reflects on the way in which Descartes conducted his work and on certain typical characteristics of his metaphysics, the more one is convinced that he was a sincere believer. A renegade would have been incapable of creating such utter havoc. If he was the intimate friend of the questionable Abbé Picot, who translated the *Principia*, if he congratulated himself on having formerly seen service in the armies of the Prince of Nassau, and had Francine baptized by a Protestant minister, all that—and a hundred other things—can be explained by the manner in which this sincerity functioned. There is no doubt that Descartes made the government of

his thought almost entirely independent of his faith, and cultivated a practical wisdom closely resembling Spinoza's. But that was the effect of an inner dislocation, an actual cleavage, not of a hypocritical attitude. His thought was not "freed," as we say, of *the* faith; it was free from *his* faith: a highly unstable solution, I admit, and subsequent history has clearly shown it.

84. Take for example the sonnet of Plantin, an excellent document on the subject of the Christian naturalism and "bourgeois" religion so widespread since the Renaissance. Taking into account the agitation which impaired this generous search for tranquillity by the fever of his devouring and restless passion for knowing and overcoming, we can say that the practical wisdom of Descartes is not very far removed from the wisdom expressed in it.

85. The expression is one used by Descartes on the subject of Balzac, who was, as he wrote to Huygens (August 1738, A.T., II, 349) "so fond of liberty that even his garters and shoulder-knots weigh heavily on him."

86. This way of looking at the humility of the laity was encouraged from time to time by certain members of the clergy. Canon Saudreau reminds us in a very interesting article on *Le mouvement antimystique en Espagne au XVIe siècle* (Revue du Clergé français, August 1, 1917) how the catechism explained to the faithful by the Dominican Carranza, then Archbishop of Toledo, was condemned by the Spanish Inquisition on the report of the well-known theologian Melchior Cano. Cano declared "reprehensible the practice of giving to the faithful religious instruction suitable only for the priests. ... He also protested vigorously against reading the Scriptures in the vernacular, and against those who made it their duty to hear confession all day long. He was very doubtful of the zeal displayed by the clergy in urging the faithful to frequent communion, and is reported to have said in one of his sermons that, in his opinion, one of the signs of the coming of the Anti-Christ was the constant frequenting of the sacraments."

87. The expression comes from Pius IX, *epist.* "Tuas libenter," ad archiepisc. Monaco-Frisingensem, December 21, 1863; Denziger-Bannwart, 1681.

88. These considerations might serve as commentary on the well-known text of Descartes (to Huygens, October 13, 1642, A.T., III, 580): "Although Religion teaches us many things on this subject (the immortality of the soul), I nevertheless acknowledge within me a weakness which, it seems to me, I have in common with most of mankind, namely: that although we should like to believe and even think we do believe most stoutly everything that Religion teaches, nevertheless we are not in the habit of being as deeply affected by the things that Faith alone teaches us, and which are beyond the reach of reason, as by those things of which we are persuaded by very evident natural reasons."

NOTES

We might note here that St. Thomas taught that the assent of faith, although *purely and simply* more certain (*simpliciter certior*) than the most perfect natural certitudes—since is rests upon God Himself—is however, less certain *with regard to us* (*quoad nos*), because it is less proportioned to our intellect (*Sum theol.*, II-II, 4, 8). Descartes perhaps had this idea in mind when he wrote Huygens the letter of consolation on the death of his wife—from which the above extract is taken. In reality, however, his thought is fundamentally different from that of St. Thomas. If, as a matter of fact, the latter says that faith is less certain than mathematics *quoad nos*, in its relation to the nature of our intellect, it is in order to explain the possibility of movements of doubt rising up against it (faith), but that does not prevent it from being *purely and simply more certain* IN US, IN NOBIS (GONET, *Clypeus*, disp. prooem., a. 5), so that we have a *more intense and more vigorous* certitude concerning the truths of faith than concerning the truths of mathematics, even though it is less in proportion to our mind and therefore *less restful* for it. *Habemus thesaurum istum in vasis fictilibus.* We may add that for St. Thomas the gifts of the Holy Spirit (which are in every Christian, as a necessity for salvation) are precisely to compensate for that disproportion, by giving our soul a kind of connaturality with things divine. The Christian, according to St. Thomas, is not like "the majority of mankind" of which Descartes speaks. He is much more "affected by the things that faith alone teaches us" than he is by those things of which natural reason convinces us. It is not reason which confirms faith, it is faith which strengthens reason in him. (See below, note 91.)

89. Cf. St. Thomas, *Sum. Theol.*, I, q. 1; John of St. Thomas, *Cursus theol., in* I. P., q. 1, disput. 8; R. Garrigou-Lagrange, *de Revelatione*, t. I, cap. 1.

90. "Habitus est lumen effective, seu per modum virtutis influens in actus cognoscitivos." John of St. Thomas, *Cursus theol., in* I, P., q. 1, disp. 2, a. 7 (Solesmes ed., p. 383).

91. St. Thomas, *Sum. theol.*, I, 12, 13: "Lumen naturale intellectus confortatur per infusionem luminis gratuiti."

92. John of St. Thomas, *Cursus theol., in* I, P., q. 1, disp. 2, a. 6 (Solesmes ed., t. I, p. 372).

93. *Ibid.*, a. 9 (t. I, 392).

94. The expression is used by Gouhier, who quite aptly points out (*loc. cit.*) that Descartes inquires of the theologians (a very laudable procedure, too) as to whether "there is any specific pronouncement in religion" (to Mersenne, A.T., I, 86) touching upon this or that question which he intends to deal with, just as he questions physicists upon the results of their experiments.

95. To Mersenne, December 1640, A.T., III, 259: "For, believing very firmly in the infallibility of the Church and being fully confident

also of my reasoning, I cannot fear that one truth will be contrary to the other." (In this letter Descartes, planning the publication of the *Principes*, asks Mersenne to sound out Cardinal de Baigné—the nuncio through whom Descares had made Bérulle's acquaintance in 1628—on the subject of "the movement of the earth, which I cannot separate from it [my philosophy] because my whole Physics depends upon it.") Cf. *epist. ad P. Dinet*, A.T., VII, 581.

96. Cf. JOHN OF ST. THOMAS, *Cursus theol., in* I. P., q. 1, disp. 2, a. 3.

97. According to the Thomists, theology will not cease in heaven; "continuabilis est cum lumine supernaturali claro, et in illud inclinat ex natura sua [. . .] quia illa scientia [subalternata] ex natura sua postulat continuari cum scientia subalternante." JOHN OF ST. THOMAS, *ibid.*, a. 5 (Solesme ed., t. I, p. 368) et a. 3 (t. I, p. 354).

98. *Discours de la Méthode*, second part, A.T., VI, 14.

99. "Et certe theologia nostris ratiociniis, quae in mathesi et aliis veritatibus adhibemus, subjicienda non est, cum nos eam capere non possimus; et quanto eam servamus simpliciorem, eo meliorem habemus." (A.T., V, 176.) Cf. A.T., II, 347.

100. "Possumus quidem et debemus demonstrare Theologicas veritates non repugnare Philosophicis, sed non debemus eas ullo modo examinare." (Burman writes *theologicas veritates*, but in this case he evidently means the verities of faith.) This text might serve as a commentary to the much more prudent one of the *Notes sur le Programme de Regius*, where Descartes writes that the theologians "devote their main study" to showing that the mysteries of faith "are not contrary to the light of reason" (A.T., VIII, second part, p. 353), but where he avoids adding the *non debemus eas ullo modo examinare*. One might add that logically Descartes should eliminate this purely negative function as well, for theology cannot acquit itself of it without claiming to acquire some knowledge of the mysteries, that is, without *in some way examining* the verities of faith, and therefore, from Descartes' point of view, without submitting these verities to the philosopher's reason. (See below, note 109.)

101. A.T., V, 176.—It is essential to recall at this point the teaching of the Council of the Vatican which, while rejecting the opinion that we find set forth by Descartes to Burman, sets up a sort of dogmatic charter of theology: "Ac ratio quidem, fide illustrata, cum sedulo, pie set sobrie quaerit, *aliquam Deo dante mysteriorum intelligentiam eamque fructuosissimam assequitur* tum ex eorum, quae naturaliter cognoscit, analogia, tum e mysteriorum ipsorum nexu inter se et cum fine hominis ultimo; nunquam tamen idonea redditur ad ea perspicienda instar veritatum, quae proprium ipsius objectum constituunt." Denz.-Bannw., 1796.

NOTES

102. MAURICE BLONDEL, *Le Christianisme de Descartes*, Revue de Métaph. et de Morale, 1896.

103. SPINOZA, *Tract. theol.-polit.*, chap. XIV, Van Vloten, II, p. 249.

104. *Ibid.*, chap. XV, p. 254.

105. Concerning the effects of the "second wave" of idealism (Kantian and post-Kantian) with regard to the theological conceptions of the Protestant schools, we read with interest Louis DALLIÈRE'S important study *Examen de l'Idealisme*, in *Etudes théologiques et Religieuses*, published in Montpellier (January-February, March-April and July-October 1931) and the review of these articles by Gabriel Marcel (*Vie Intellectuelle*, March 10, 1932).

106. A.T., V, 176.

107. Preface to the French translation of the *Principia*, A.T., IX, second part, 18.

108. "Which has been so subjected to Aristotle that it is impossible to explain another philosophy without making it seem contrary to faith." A.T., I, 85-86; to Mersenne, December 18, 1629.—Cf. the second letter to Father Mesland on the Eucharist (1645 or 1646) : "It seems to me we must be careful to distinguish the opinions decided upon by the Church from those commonly accepted by Doctors and which are *founded upon an uncertain Physics*." (A.T., IV, 347.)

109. See above, p. 108; *Entretien avec Burman*, A.T., V, 176. Descartes does not realize that this purely negative function would itself be impossible without an effort to acquire some knowledge of the mysteries (and in fact he devoted himself without much success to just such an effort with regard to the mystery of the Eucharist). To the very extent that he thus continues to believe, in spite of his basic inclinations, in a theology as science, however reduced its rôle may be, he is forced, we must not forget, to regard this theology, this negative defense of dogmas, as subordinated to philosophy, and as being no more than an application of philosophy—his own, of course, not any longer that of Aristotle—to revealed data. When in 1648 he said to Burman: *"Et si sciret auctor aliquem ex sua Philosophia ratiocinia deducturum in Theologia, et in eum modum sua Philosophia abusurum, eum operae suae poeniteret,"* he was forgetting his letters to Mesland on the Eucharist and what he wrote in 1638 to Father Vatier, in 1641 to Mersenne and in 1642 to Father Dinet: "and I shall also say that after all, I have no fear whatsoever that anything can be found in it [his metaphysics] against faith; for on the contrary, I make so bold as to say that *never has faith been so strongly supported by human reasons, as it can be if my principles are followed;* and particularly Transubstantiation, which the Calvinists maintain cannot be explained by ordinary Philosophy, *is very easily explained by mine."* (To Father Vatier, February 22, 1638, A.T., I, p. 564. Very easily indeed! He speaks of it as he would of a puzzle or a problem in geometry . . .) *"You will see* (in the

answer to Arnauld) *that what is set forth by the Councils concerning the Blessèd Sacrament is so consistent with my philosophy that I claim it cannot possibly be explained correctly by the commonly-accepted philosophy;* so much so that I believe the latter would have been rejected as repugnant to faith if mine had been known first. And I swear to you in all seriousness that I believe this, just as I have written it. For this reason I did not wish to keep silent about it, so that I might beat with their own weapons those who mix Aristotle with the Bible, and seek to take advantage of the authority of the Church in order to give play to their passions—I mean people like those who had Galileo condemned and who would like to have my opinions condemned in like manner, if they could accomplish it; but if it is ever a question of that I shall undertake to show that there is no opinion in their Philosophy that accords so well with faith, as my own opinions do." (To Mersenne, March 31, 1641, A.T., III, 349-350.) "Omnino profiteor nihil ad religionem pertinere, quod non aeque ac etiam magis facile explicetur per mea principia, quam per ea, quae vulgo recepta sunt. Jamque hujus rei mihi videor specimen dedisse satis luculentum, in fine meae responsionis ad quartas Objectiones, circa quaestionem in qua omnium difficillime Philosophia cum Theologia solet conciliari. Et idem in aliis quibuslibet, si opus sit, praestare paratus sum, ac etiam ostendere multa e contra esse in vulgari Philosophia, quae revera pugnant cum iis quae in Theologia sunt certa, etsi id vulgo a Philosophis dissimuletur, vel ob longam iis credendi consuetudinem non advertatur." (*Letter to Father Dinet*, A.T., VII, 581.)

110. To Mersenne, A.T., III, 350.

111. DE WULF, *Bull. de la Soc. granc. de Philosophie*, June 1914.

112. ST. THOMAS, *de Verit.*, q. 9, a. 1; q. 11, a. 3, ad 12.

113. JOHN OF ST. THOMAS, *Curs. theol., in* II-II, q. 1, disp. 2, a. 1 (Vivès, t. VII, p. 31-33): "Dicendum demonstrationem philosophi esse certiorem actualiter ex conjunctione ad fidem, nec posse demonstrantem intellectum, etiam postquam cessavit demonstratio, et visio, elicere actum fidei circa eamdem veritatem jam visam.

. . . Ita ergo philosophandum est in fide, quae est lumen superius ad scientiam naturalem, ex conjunctione enim ad fidem operatur scientia demonstrationem certam non solum certitudine sibi propria, sed etiam superaddita, et participata a fide, sicut Angelus inferior intelligit melius ex illuminatione superioris, quam ex sola propria virtute, nec tamen ista certitudo participatur in scientia omni eo modo quo est in fide, quia non est capax obscuritatis, sed solum certitudinis . . . Illa certitudo derivata a fide supernaturalis manet."

114. "Those who read the works of this learned man [. . .] will feel an inward joy at being born in a century and in a country fortunate enough to save us the trouble of seeking in bygone ages among the pagans, and at the ends of the earth among Barbarians and foreigners,

NOTES

a doctor to instruct us in truth, or rather a monitor faithful enough to incline us to become instructed in it." MALEBRANCHE, *Rech. de la Vér.,* VI, conclusion to the last three books. Thus the Christianity of the seventeenth century had a much less ample conception of itself and its relations to the entire human effort, than that of the early centuries and of St. Justin.

The desire for a philosophy which owes nothing to pagan antiquity also seems to be one of the motives for the all-out criticism levelled against Aristotle by Father Laberthonnière and, after him, by Jacques Chevalier.

115. To Princess Elizabeth, June 28, 1643, A.T., III, 692-693.

116. Father Laberthonnière has stressed at great length this reversal, especially in a communication to the Société française de Philosophie (*Bull. de la Soc. fr. de Phil.,* June 1914).

All the significant points of the present work were already drawn up when I learned of Laberthonnière's studies on Descartes; it is a case of spontaneous encounter which is all the more intriguing to point out as it cannot be ascribed to any doctrinal prejudice we are likely to be sharing.

117. "The Church has within herself enemies more violent than the heretics," wrote Leibnitz on another occasion (first letter to Arnauld— Grotefend, *Briefwechsel zw. Leibnitz, Arnauld, u. dem Landgrafen von Hessen-Rheinfels,* Hanover, 1846), "It is to be feared that the latest heresy may be, if not atheism, at least an avowed naturalism." Leibnitz probably is thinking here not of Descartes, but of the Cartesians and the Baconians.

118. Letter of May 21, 1687, to the Marquis d'Allemans.

119. Cf. ST. THOMAS, *Contra Gent.,* I, 4 (Cf. *Compendium theologiae,* cap. 36)—confirmed by the Council of the Vatican; GONET, *de Gratia,* disp. I, n. 1, §4; BILLUART, *de Gratia,* diss. III, a. 2, §1; GARRIGOU-LAGRANGE, *de Revelatione,* t. I, pp. 411-415.

120. Preface to the French translation of the *Principia.* A.T., IX, part 2, 18: "The last and most important consequence of these principles is that one can, by cultivating them, acquire in time *a perfect knowledge of all philosophy* and rise to *the highest degree of wisdom."—Inventum philosophicum* SEMPER *est perfectibile,* the ancients used to say . . .

Concerning the notion of Christian philosophy I explained my stand in a communication to the Société française de Philosophie (cf. *Bulletin,* March-June 1931), which I hope to take up again and finish. It is not only through the proposing of objects (accessible in themselves to natural reason, but which in fact, natural reason alone fails to grasp or impairs), it is also because it modifies the internal dynamism of the activities of the subject (as we have seen above, pp. 122-123, concerning the strengthening of philosophy by faith and by theology) and because it centers these activities above philosophy, that faith brings the philosophical *habitus* to a state of integrity which surpasses the power of the forces of reason alone.

A valuable historical elucidation of this problem is found in the work of Etienne GILSON, *L'Esprit de la Philosophie Mediévale*, Paris, Vrin, 1932.

121. Preface to the French translation of the *Principia*, A.T., IX, 2nd part, 2.

122. *Ibid.*, A.T., IX, 2nd part, 14.

123. Clerselier. Cf. BAILLET, *Vie*, I, 115; II, 282-283.

124. Preface to the French translation of the *Principia*, A.T., IX, 2nd part, 8.

124. E. BOUTROUX, *Du Rapport de la morale à la science dans la philosophie de Descartes* (Rev. de Mét. et de Mor., 1896).

126. Id., *ibid.*

127. Cf. ST. THOMAS, *Sum. theol.*, I-II, 19, 4: "Quod autem ratio humana sit regula voluntatis humanae, ex qua ejus bonitas mensuretur, habet ex lege aeterna, quae est ratio divina . . . Unde manifestum est, quod multo magis dependet bonitas voluntatis humanae a lege aeterna, quam a ratione humana; et ubi deficit humana ratio, oportet ad rationem aeternam recurrere." We know that in the doctrine of Descartes (theory of the eternal truths depending on the sole *will* of God), this notion of eternal law disappears.

128. Mgr. CHOLLET, article *Descartes* in the Dict. de Théologie Vacant-Mangenot.

129. Lucien ROURE, *Doctrines et Problèmes*, Paris, 1900.

130. Address at the Sorbonne for the tercentenary of Descartes, 1896.

131. ". . . the grandeur *of all created things* . . ." It is by that grandeur that God makes us love Him. How can we fail to think of the *natura naturans* and the *natura naturata* of the *Ethics*?

132. To Chanut, Feb. 1st, 1647, A.T., IV, 607-609. It will be noted that to love God "so perfectly that we desire nothing more in the world except that His will be done," is indeed to love God efficaciously *super omnia.*

133. It would be a great mistake to deny the possibility of a *natural love* by which God is loved as the Author of nature, and which is distinct from the *gratuitous* or supernatural love (or from *charity*), by which God is loved as the Author of eternal life (Denz.-Bannw., 1034, 1036). But it is impossible, as St. Thomas teaches, that *in the state of fallen nature* this natural love be capable of making us love God *efficaciously above all things*, for that would imply that nature has not been *wounded* by original sin, and that the forces of free will have not been *weakened* by that sin, as the Church has defined it. (Denz.-Bannw., 181, 199, 793). Cr. *Sum. theol.*, I-II, 109, 3.

134. Cf. above, p. 19: "The true principles by which one can reach

NOTES

the highest degree of wisdom, in which the *sovereign good of human life* consists, are those which I have set forth in this book." Preface to the French translation of the *Principia*, A.T., IX, 2nd part, 9.

135. St. Thomas, *Sum. theol.*, I, 1, 3, ad 2.

136. Cf. J. M., *Trois Réformateurs*, chap. II, note 50 (new French edition); *Réflexions sur l'Intelligence*, chap. II.

137. *IIIe Médit.*, A.T., IX, 33.

138. Cf. the texts referred to in note 50 of *Trois Réformateurs* (new French edition).

"By the noun *thought* I mean everything which is so much within us that we are immediately conscious of it (*ut ejus immediate conscii simus*). Thus all the operations of the will, the understanding, the imagination and of the senses are thoughts" (*Rép. aux secondes objections*, A.T., VII, 160; IX, 124).

"By the word 'thought' I mean everything which happens within us in such a way that we perceive it immediately by ourselves (*quae nobis consciis in nobis fiunt, quatenus eorum in nobis conscientia est*):' that is why not only understanding, willing, imagining but also feeling is the same thing, in this case, as thinking." (*Principes*, I, 9.)

Thus thought is the only object which thought itself "immediately perceives."

"By the noun *idea* I mean that form of each one of our thoughts, through the immediate perception of which we have knowledge *of those same thoughts, per cujus immediatam perceptionem ipsius ejusdem cogitationis conscius sum.*" (A.T., VII, 160; IX, 124).

Our thought "finds in itself, first of all, the *ideas* of several things; and as long as it *simply contemplates* them and does not assert that there is anything outside itself which is like those ideas, and as long as it does not deny it, it is in no danger of being mistaken." (*Principes*, I, 13.)

"There is nothing more in conformity with reason than to believe that the spirit newly-joined to the body of an infant is occupied solely in feeling or confusedly perceiving *the ideas* of pain, tickling, heat, cold, and the like . . ." (to XXX, August 1641, A.T., III, 424).

"So that natural light makes me know with the force of evidence that *ideas are in me like pictures or images* which, in truth, can easily fall from the perfection of the things from which they are drawn, but which can never contain anything greater or more perfect." (*Médit. III*, A.T., IX, 33.)

"I speak of the *idea*, which is never outside of the understanding, and in respect to which 'to be objectively' means nothing more than 'to reside in the understanding' in the way *objects* usually reside in it." (*Rép. aux premières objections*, A.T., IX, 82.)

"I have often pointed out that I take the noun 'idea' for everything immediately conceived by the mind, *pro omni eo quod immediate a mente percipitur . . ."* (*Rép. aux troisièmes objections*, A.T., VII, 181.)

To these texts can be added the following, quoted in the *Vocabulaire philosophique* by Lalande: "Some [of my thoughts] are like the images of things, and the noun *ideas* fits them and them alone; as when I picture to myself a man, a chimera, or an angel, or even God. Others, in addition, have other forms, as when I will, I fear, I affirm or I deny . . . And of this sort of thought, some are called wills or affections and others judgments." (*Troisième Médit.*, §5.)

"Between these forms (figures) . . . it is not those which are imprinted in the exterior sense organs . . . but only those which are traced upon the surface of the H gland, where the seat of the imagination and of common sense is found, which must be taken for *ideas*, that is to say, for the *forms or representations* that the *rational* soul will immediately consider when, being united to this machine, it will imagine or feel some object." (*Traité de l'Homme*, §70.)

Cf. E. GILSON, *Etudes sur le rôle de la pensée médiévale dans la formation du système cartésien* (Paris, Vrin, 1930, in particular Part I, chapter I, and Part II, chapter III); and *Commentaire sur le Discours de la Méthode* (Paris, Vrin, 1925, in particular pp. 318-323).

139. In Malebranche the representative idea 'emigrates' so to speak, from our thought to God Himself, in Whom it is seen; and there is left in us only our *perceptions* of these *ideas*. (*Réponse à Regis*, chap. II, n. 14). Cf. H. GOUHIER, *La Philosophie de Malebranche*, Paris, Vrin, 1926, Part III, chapter II.

140. *Rép. aux troisièmes objections*, A.T., VII, 181.

141. Compare the texts quoted in Appendix I of my book *Les Degrés du Savoir*. It is advisable to refer in particular to the theory of divine ideas in St. Bonaventure and especially in Duns Scotus, in seeking the Scholastic sources of the Cartesian notion of ideas. (For Duns Scotus, divine ideas were *ipsa objecta ab aeterno a Deo intellecta*.) See also below, note 196.

142. Thus is dispelled the obscurity of which Lalande's *Vocabulaire* (I, p. 331 a) complains in the explanation given by Descartes (in his replies to Hobbes) concerning "the origin of the meaning he attributes" to the word "idea." This explanation is not obscure; it reveals a very remarkable filiation. As to the "forms (figures) . . . traced on the surface of the H gland, where the seat of the imagination and of common sense is found" (*Treatise on Man*, §70), they should be considered as the physical counterpart of the ideas which the soul contemplates *in itself* when it imagines or feels some object.

143. Cf. *Principes*, I, 66-70.

144. Cf. J. M., *Réflexions sur l'Intelligence*, p. 74-75.

145. Cf. IIIe *Médit.*, A.T., IX, 27 ff.

146. "It came to my mind that perhaps some God had given me

such a nature that I might be mistaken even with regard to things which seemed to me most evident . . ." *Médit.* III, A.T., IX, 28.

For the same reason Descartes, before he had established the existence of God and of divine veracity, also questions the "demonstrations of mathematics and its principles (*etiam de iis principiis, quae hactenus putavimus esse per se nota*)." *Principes*, I, 5.—One sees by this passage that if the Cartesian doubt bears first of all on the propositions concerning the existential order, it is quite true that in the background it bears also upon propositions of an essential order, and even on first principles (at least in so far as we are not in the act of considering them.)

147. *IIIe Médit.*, A.T., IX, 37.

148. In the *third Méditation*, the first Cartesian proof is primarily founded upon the idea of the infinite; in the *Principes* it is upon the idea of the perfect. Descartes takes, right from the start, as an innate idea, the idea of God elaborated through centuries of philosophy and theology; that is why for him it is a matter of course that *infinite* and *perfect* are identical in God, and can be used interchangeably to designate Him. On the convergence of *infinite* and *perfect* in Christian metaphysics, see the important chapter in *L'Esprit de la Philosophie médiévale* by E. GILSON, Paris, Vrin, 1932, vol. I, chap. III. He restates a question on which KOYRÉ'S remarks (*Essai sur l'idée de Dieu et les preuves de son existence chez Descartes*, Paris, Ernest Leroux, 1922, pp. 5-13, 125-128) did not always do justice to the Mediaevals.

149. Thus one must agree with O. HAMELIN (*Le Système de Descartes*, p. 199)—against the interpretation given by LIARD (ed. of the *Principes*, p. 102) and partially against that given by KOYRÉ (Essai, p. 159-160)— that the real step taken by Descartes in this first argument consists in arriving by means of causality at the conclusion that the idea of God has a *real ideate*. But the proof constantly assumes that this idea is the image of a *possible* ideate.

150. *Réponse aux premières objections*, A.T., IX, 83.

151. *Abrégé en tête des Médit.*, A.T., IX, 11.

152. *Principes*, I, 17.

153. To Mersenne, May 2, 1644, A.T., IV, 111.

154. *Rép. aux premières objections*, A.T., IX, 86. Descartes thus arrives at a cause which "having the virtue of being and existing in itself, must certainly also have all those perfections, the ideas of which it conceives."

155. *IIIe Médit.*, A.T., IX, 41.

156. Cf. ST. THOMAS, *Sum. theol.*, I, 2, 2 ad 2: "In the demonstration of cause by effect, it is necessary to use the effect in place of the definition of the cause in order to prove the latter's existence; and this is particularly true as regards God; for, in order to prove that something exists it is necessary to take as *medium*, the signification of the noun,

and not the essence (*quid significet nomen, non autem quod quid est*), because the question *quid est* comes after the question *an est.* Now the nouns attributed to God are attributed to Him in virtue of His effects; that is why in demonstrating the existence of God by His effects we can take as *medium* the significations of this noun 'God.'"

157. "It seems to me, however, that all these demonstrations taken from effects . . . are not accomplished . . . if we do not unite with them the idea we have of God. For, my soul being finite, I cannot know that the order of causes is not infinite, except in so far as I have within me this idea of the primary cause. And although one admits a primary cause which preserves me, I cannot say that it is God, *if I have not truly the idea of God.*" To Mersenne, May 2, 1644, A.T., IV, 111.

158. ". . . What I hinted at in my reply to the first objections, but only in a word or two, in order not to make light of the reasons of others, who commonly admit that *non datur progressus in infinitum.* And I, for one, do not admit it; on the contrary, I believe that *datur revera talis progressus in divisione partium materiae*, as will be seen in my Traité de Philosophie which has just been printed." *Ibid.*

In *Etudes sur le rôle de la pensée médiévale dans la formation du système cartésien*, by E. GILSON, pp. 207 ff., we find a more detailed discussion of Descartes' position with regard to *progressus in infinitum.* This chapter was already written when I learned of Gilson's studies on the Cartesian proofs of the existence of God (*op. cit.*, P. II, chap. III, IV, V). I am glad to note that in a general way my own intepretation of these proofs agrees with his.

159. *Sum. theol.*, I, 46, 2.

160. Cf. the opuscule *de Aeternitate Mundi, ad fin.*: "Et praeterea adhuc non est demonstratum, quod Deus non possit facere, quod sint infinita actu."

161. *Cf. IIIe Médit.*, A.T., IX, 39 ff.

162. *Sum. theol.*, I, 104, 1, ad 4.

163 *Rép. aux quatrièmes objections*, A.T., IX, 190. Cf. *IIIe Médit.*, A.T., IX, 39; and the letter to Mersenne, January 28, 1641: "I maintain that we have ideas not only of all that which is in our intellect, but even of all that which is in the will. For we cannot will anything without knowing that we will it, nor can we know it except through an idea. But I do not set down that this idea is different from action itself." (A.T., III, 295.)

164. *Rép. aux premières objections*, A.T., IX, 88.

-65. *Rép. aux quatrièmes objections*, A.T., IX, 182. See below note 171.

166. *Principes*, I, 37.

167. "And it is true that the simple consideration of such a being leads us so easily to the knowledge of its existence, that conceiving God is almost the same thing as conceiving that He exists. But that does

not prevent the idea that we have of God or of a supremely perfect
Being from being vastly different from this proposition: God exists;
and does not prevent the one from serving as means or antecedent to
prove the other." (To Mersenne, July 1641, A.T., III, 396.) And
again: "All the knowledge that we can have of God without miracle
in this life comes from reasoning and from progress in our discursive
reasoning." (To the Marquis of Newcastle, March or April 1648, A.T.,
V, 136.)

168. Ve Medit., A.T., IX, 51.

169. Ibid., A.T., IX, 52.

For Descartes, existence is quite certainly a perfection; passages
quoted by Koyré himself (Essai, p. 178) clearly confirm that. On this
point Descartes has neither rejected nor modified what he received
from traditional teaching.

On the other hand, it is clear to whoever considers things according
to their own nature and not according to modern prejudice, that no
analytical process consists in verifying a simple fact of logical con-
taining (subsumption), but indeed in seeing an intelligible exigency: and
it is that very thing one means to signify in saying that one term is
contained in the notion of the other. That is why the problem set
concerning the ontological argument by HANNEQUIN (Essais, II, p. 260)
and by KOYRÉ (op. cit., p. 177-178) can be held to be a pseudo-problem.

170. Ibid., A.T., IX, 53.

171. Sum. theol., I, 2, 1, ad 2.

In his replies to Caterus (A.T., VII, 115-117; IX, 91) Descartes
has completely (and knowingly, it seems) misunderstood the Anselmian
argument as it is presented here by St. Thomas, and at the same time,
St. Thomas's criticism of this argument. He acts as though it were
only a question of the noun 'God' and not of the notion of God, and as
though this argument criticized by St. Thomas were a simple tautology.
In reality, the logical process of St. Anselm is already that of Descartes, and it is the very problem set by the Cartesian argument that
St. Thomas deals with in advance here.

Concerning the historical filiation of St. Anselm to Descartes, we
concur in Gilson's conclusions (Etudes, p. 42, and P. II, chap. IV); it
seems probable that Descartes did not read the Proslogion and knew
the argument of St. Anselm only through its refutation by St. Thomas
(although Mersenne could have served here as intermediary; cf. KOYRÉ,
Essai, p. 185 ff.).

With regard to the intrinsic significance of the argument, it is obvious
that the logical movement is the same in St. Anselm and in Descartes.
Yet the personal note remains, in my opinion, very different. St.
Anselm's argument is the argument of a contemplator, it is born in
prayer; and if philosophically it is without demonstrative value, psy-
chologically it seems like a kind of anticipation—in a mind which already

knows God by faith, and which lives in faith—of a more luminous knowledge, apperception making felt what absurdity it would be for such a Being not to exist. The misfortune has been to try to express and to justify this apperception rationally. Descartes' argument is also the argument of a great intuitive, but an intuitive geometrician. It has a definitely rationalist value which is absent in the argument of St. Anselm.

On the other hand the Cartesian proof is not long in becoming orientated (*Rép. aux I^{es} Obj.*, A.T., IX, 94) toward that *infinite power* by which God is in a way cause of Himself and which we have met in connection with the second proof of the *Meditations*. Is that an essential exigency of the ontological argument as Descartes means it? Is it an additional explanation by which Descartes falls back into a system of ideas conceived from another source? In any case, Gilson is right in remarking (*Etudes*, P. II, ch. V) that the idea of God thus introduced into modern metaphysics is new in relation to St. Anselm as well as to St. Thomas Aquinas.

Everything happens as though the clear and distinct idea of the perfect Being was already assuring the philosopher that this Being enjoyed at least possible existence (cf. below, note 208) itself conceived (cf. above, p. 223, and note 196) as a beginning of actual existence. From then on the consideration of the *infinite power* of such a being will suffice to show that it enjoys an existence truly and fully actual: "When, because we cannot think that His existence is possible without at the same time taking into account His infinite power, knowing that He can exist by His own force, we conclude from that that He really exists, and that He has been from all eternity." (A.T., IX, 94; cf. *to Mersenne*, March 4, 1641, III, 329-331). Thus, for Descartes, the idea of God makes us become aware, so to speak, of the way in which He constitutes Himself in being.

Let us add that the existence of God—if it is absolutely necessary, of a necessity of nature, so that God is absolutely not *free* not to exist— is however not necessary in the way in which a geometric essence, to suppose the impossible, would exist *a se;* that would be falling into univocity. For divine existence is at the same time supremely *voluntary*, the act of will, by which God wills and loves His own goodness, being in fact that same nature or essence by which He exists. Here we are confronted with that fundamental distinction of the *voluntary* and the *free* that the Scholastics had explained in so profound a manner, and the forgetting of which has involved the moderns in so many difficulties. And at the same time we understand that the concept of aseity is not a *logical* or *geometrical* concept, neither an entirely positive concept as Descartes would have it, nor completely negative as some of his Scholastic adversaries seemed to understand it, but an analogical and positivo-negative concept, *metaphysical* and transcendental. These remarks do

NOTES

justice to the truth Scotus and Descartes hit upon (in a very different way, however, for Scotus remains far from the idea of a God *causa sui*) although thinking it in conceptual forms that are contestable and erroneous.

172. *Commentary in Sum. theol.*, I, 2, 1, ad 2.

173. *Commentary* in I, 82, 3.

174. *Sum. theol.*, I, 2, 1. On the meaning and the implications of this assertion see chapter V and appendix II of my work *Les Degrés du Savoir*.

175. *Sum theol.*, I, 2, 1; I-II, 94, 2; *De Verit.*, q. 10, a 12; *in I. Sent.*, dist. 3, q. 1, a. 2.

176. *De Verit.*, q. 10, a. 12. This is so whether the predicate forms part of the essence of the subject or whether the subject is implied, as proper subject, in the notion of the predicate. On the *per se primo modo* and the *per se secundo modo*, cf. *Réflexions sur l'Intelligence*, pp. 71, 72.

177. *De Verit.*, *ibid.*

178. It is equally remarkable that, to give to the Cartesian *cogito* its absolutely full meaning, according to which thought attains itself not by a reflex knowledge, but as primary object directly attained, then the *cogito* is applicable only to God Himself: "ante ipsum intelligere [divinum] no praesupponitur aliud objectum directe cognitum, quia non praesupponitur aliud quo constituatur natura divina, et ita cum sit primum objectum divinae intellectionis ipsummet intelligere, non reflexe, sed directe ipsum cognoscit." JOHN OF ST. THOMAS, *Curs. theol.*, I. P. q. 12, disp. 15, a. 3 (Vivès, t. II, p. 352).

179. *Ecclesiastes*, IX, 4.

180. *Critique of Pure Reason, Transcendental Dialectic*, book II, chap. III, section 5, *The Impossibility of a cosmological proof of the existence of God.*

181. To Mersenne, May 27, 1638, A.T., II, 138.

182. *Answer for Arnauld*, July 29, 1648, A.T., V, 223-224 (transl.).

183. "I frankly admit that there are self-contradictions which are so evident that we cannot bring them before our minds without considering them to be entirely impossible, like the one you propose: *that God might have ordained it that creatures be not dependent on Him.* But, in order to know the immensity of His power, we must keep from bringing them before our minds." To Mesland, May 2, 1644, A.T., IV, 119. Cf. St. Thomas on these questions, *Sum. theol.*, I, 25, 3 and 4; *Sum. contra Gent.*, I, 84; II, 22-25.

184. To Mersenne, May 6, 1630, A.T., I, 149-150.

185. To Mersenne, April 15, 1630, A.T., I, 145.

186. *Ibid.*

187. To Mersenne (?), May 27, 1630 (?), A.T., I, 151-152.

188. *Ibid.*, p. 152-153.

189. It seems that on still another point a logical filiation from Vasquez to Descartes can be discerned: Vasquez's theory of the objective concept prepares for the Cartesian notion of ideas. Cf. my *Réflexions sur l'Intelligence*, pp. 32, 33.

190. VASQUEZ, *Comment. et Disput, in Iam Partem Sti Thomae*, disp. 50, cap. 6, *Nullam creaturam ex vi visionis Dei, sed peculiari revelatione videri, verior sententia est.* Cf. JOHN OF ST. THOMAS, *Curs. theol.*, I. P., q. 12, disp. 15, a. 3, Vivès, t. II, p. 339.

191. To Mersenne(?), 27th of May, 1630(?), A.T., I, p. 152.—The passages quoted by A. KOYRÉ, *Essai*, p. 20-21, do not prove that Descartes had ever modified that doctrine, which for him is absolutely fundamental.

192. JOHN OF ST. THOMAS, *Cursus theol.*, in I. P., q. 12, disp. 15, a. 3, Vivès, t. II, p. 342.—It is disappointing that in his otherwise admirable study on *La Structure métaphysique du concret selon saint Thomas d'Aquin* (Paris, Vrin, 1931), Aimé FOREST did not bring out the thought of St. Thomas on this point with sufficient clearness. For St. Thomas, the possibles as such as so far from proceeding "from a *will* which *freely* constitutes them in accordance with wisdom," (*op. cit.*, p. 153) that they cannot be, in so far as they are possibles, objects of the love of God. Loves means order to existence: as soon as God loves, He causes to exist. (Cf. JOHN OF ST. THOMAS, *ibid., in* I. P. q. 19, disp. 4, a. 6, n. 12 and ff., Vivès, t. III, p. 282 and ff.). It is in so far as He gives *to creatures He causes to exist* all that their nature demands and "all that they need to attain their end in the ensemble of the universe," that the work of God pertains to wisdom and will joined together, "to liberality, charity and creative knowledge."

193. Cf. R. GARRIGOU-LAGRANGE, *La Première Donnée de l'Intelligence*, in Mélanges thomistes, 1923.

194. "Dicere autem quod ex simplici voluntate dependeat justitia, est dicere quod divina voluntas non procedat secundum ordinem sapientiae, quod est blasphemum." ST. THOMAS, *De Veritate*, q. 23, a. 6.— Leibnitz too will say that that is "dishonoring" God: "Why then could He not be the evil principle of the Manicheans as well as the good principle of the orthodox?" *Théodicée*, II, §§176 and 177.

195. Cf. the interesting article by Roland DALBIEZ: *Les Sources scolastiques de la théorie cartésienne de l'être objectif*, Revue d'histoire de la philosophie, October-December, 1929.

196. "Scotus enim . . . putat quod esse cognitum, repraesentatum et quicquid aliud aequivalet, est esse quoddam distinctum contra esse in rerum natura: non tamen est apud eum esse essentiae, sed potius esse secundum quid, et essentiae, et existentiae rerum . . . et in tali esse ponit omnia alia a Deo produci per actum intellectus divini . . . S. Thomas autem docuit chimaericum hoc esse." CAJETAN, *in Sum. theol.*, I, 14, 5.

"Scotus [*in I Sent.*, dist. 35 et 36, Vivès, t. X, p. 533-587] determinat quod *esse cognitum* non est esse reale absolutum, aut respectivum, nec est esse relativum secundum rationem, sed est *esse diminutum* rei, sive absolute, sive relative; quod vocatur esse secundum quid; ita quod res habens talem modum essendi, fundat relationem rationis ad intellectum: putatque lapidem, etc., *entia producta esse ab aeterno a Deo per actum* intellectus divini in tali esse, et hujusmodi entia *secundum quid esse et vocari ideas* . . .

Ego autem peripatetico lacte eductus, ac in aere, ut aiunt, loqui nesciens, praeter latitudinem entis realis solum ens rationis novi (5 et 6 Met.). Ens autem rationis relationem aut negationem didici a sancto Thoma in q. disp. de Ver., q. 21, a. 1. Unde cum esse objectivum non sit modus essendi secundum rem, neque sit negatio, restat, quod sit esse relativum secundum rationem in communi loquendo." *Ibid., in* I, 15, 1 (*An sint ideae.*)

R. Dalbiez (art cit.) has very clearly shown the significance of these paragraphs. We might add that on still another point Cartesian theodicy seems to depend on the Scotist tradition. Scotus had divine essence consist formally in *radical infinity*. That conception must have played an important part in the formation of Descartes' thought.

197. *Principes*, II, 36 and 37.

198. "Descartes here is no longer simply advising abstention from a difficult and hazardous search, he definitely warns against searching for what does not exist. Properly speaking, the pursuit of God's ends is a pursuit without object. If he does not wish us to give our attention to final causes, it is because in virtue of the particular conception he has of the freedom of God, he thinks he can demonstrate that God never acts in view of an end. "E. GILSON, *La Doctrine cartésienne de la Liberté et la théologie*, Paris, 1915, p. 93.

A. KOYRÉ (*Essai*, p. 18 and ff.) holds the opposite opinion. He is certain that passages are not lacking where Descartes speaks of "the order of eternal Providence" (*Principes*, I, 40). But the question is whether these texts do not remain somewhat exoteric in relation to the deeper thought of the philosopher. And we might add that even in this article of the *Principia*, and in the following article, it is expressly a question of the *power* of God, not of His intelligence or His wisdom. It is by His *"omnipotence"* that God "has not only known from all eternity that which is or can be, but has also willed it [*voluit ac praeordinavit*]" (*ibid.*, I, 41). The passages of the letter [to Mersenne?] and of the letter to Mesland quoted below (note 199) present a principle from which a pure and simple refusal to admit that God acts in view of a purpose, follows logically.

On this question, see below, note 202.

199. "For in God, it is one and the same thing to will, to understand and to create, without having one precede the other, *ne quidem ratione*." To Mersenne(?), May 27, 1630(?), A.T., I, 152.—"*We . . . should not . . .*

conceive any preference [precedence?] or priority between His understanding and His will." To Father Mesland, May 2, 1644, A.T., IV, p. 119.

Neither did the nominalists of the Occam school admit any distinction even of reason merely conceptual (*distinctio rationis*) between the divine perfections, unless it were a verbal distinction (*rationis ratiocinantis*), as between Tullius and Cicero. That was to destroy by the root the very possibility of using our concepts in order to arrive at a philosophical or theological knowledge of things divine. (Cf. R. GARRIGOU-LAGRANGE, *Dieu, son existence et sa nature*, 5th ed., pp. 350 ff.). This time Descartes is in historical dependence not on Scotus, but on the nominalists.

On the historical relations of Descartes to Duns Scotus and to the Nominalists, see KOYRÉ'S interesting discussion, *Essai*, pp. 61-118 and GILSON, *Etudes*, pp. 24-25, 225-229. It will be very difficult to accomplish the unravelling of all the influences Descartes came under because it was in the eclectic syncretism characteristic of the "baroque period" that Descartes knew Scholasticism, through his masters at La Flèche as through Suarez or Vasquez. Such syncretism furthermore presented to so demanding a mind a Scholasticism which was, truth to tell, defenseless.

200. "Nam ego eodem modo statui, omnia inevitabili necessitate ex Dei natura sequi, ac omnes statuunt, ex Dei natura sequi, quod se ipsum intelligit." SPINOZA, *Epist.* 43, Van Vloten and Land, t. III, p. 160.

201. "Sed aeternitas est simul et semel?—Hoc concipi non potest. Est quidem simul et semel, quatenus Dei naturae nunquam quid additur aut ab ea quid detrahitur. Sed non est simul et semel, quatenus simul existit; nam cum possimus in ea distinguere partes jam post mundi creationem, quidni etiam possemus facere ante eam, cum eadem duratio sit? Ea autem jam creaturis, e.g. per quinque annorum millia coextensa fuit et cum iis duravit, et sic etiam potuisset fuisse, si ante mundi creationem mensuram habuissemus." (GÖTTINGEN *Ms.*, A.T., V, 148-149.)

202. "Omnes Dei fines nos latent et temerarium est in eos involare velle . . . Sed nos hic maxime erramus. *Concipimus Deum tanquam magnum aliquem hominem, qui hoc et hoc sibi proponit, et eo his et his mediis tendit, quod certe Deo maxime indignum.*" *Ibid.*, A.T., V, 158.— St. Thomas, in showing that God acts for an end, because He has wisdom, had nevertheless explained that the will of God *is not subject to any kind of causality*: "Si aliquis uno actu velit finem, et alio actu, ea quae sunt ad finem, velle finem erit ei causa volendi ea quae sunt ad finem; sed si unio actu velit finem, et ea, quae sunt ad finem, hoc esse non potest: quia idem non est causa suiipsius. Et tamen erit verum dicere, quod velit ordinare ea quae sunt ad finem, in finem. Deus autem, sicut uno actu omnia in essentia sua intelligit, uno actu vult

218

NOTES

omnia in sua bonitate. Unde, sicut in Deo intelligere causam non est causa intelligendi effectus, sed ipse intelligit effectus in causa; ita velle finem non est ei causa volendi ea quae sunt ad finem: sed tamen vult ea, quae sunt ad finem, ordinari in finem. Vult ergo hoc esse propter hoc; sed non propter hoc vult hoc . . . Voluntas Dei rationabilis est, non quod aliquid sit Deo causa volendi, sed inquantum vult unum esse propter aliud. ST. THOMAS, *Sum. theol.*, I, 19, 5, corp. et ad 1.

203. Cf. *Discours de la Méthode*, Pt. IV, A.T., VI, 35; *Principes*, I, 19 et 22; *Göttingen Ms.*, A.T., V, 158.

204. T. L. PENIDO, *Le Rôle de l'Analogie en Théologie dogmatique*, Paris, Vrin, 1931, pp. 20, 21. It is hardly necessary to call attention to the fact that the word "anthropomorphic" is taken here, and all through our discussion, in the strictly technical sense and not in the much wider meaning Gilson gives it in *L'Esprit de la Philosophie Médiévale*, t. I, chap. V.

205. *Médit. V*, A.T., IX, 54.

206. I agree with A. KOYRÉ on this point (*Essai*, p. 177). See also the *réponses aux premières objections*, A.T., IX, 93.

207. *Médit. V*, A.T., IX, 53 ff.

208. *Rép. aux premières objections*, A.T., IX, 92. Cf. A. KOYRÉ, *Essai*, p. 143. It is well known that according to the Thomists the proposition "God is possible" is not evident *for us* (as Descartes believed it) nor demonstrable *a priori* (as Leibnitz believed). "Leibnitz, like Descartes, can only demonstrate one thing, that is, that we do not see any impossibility in God's existing; the positive possibility escapes us, and will escape us as long as we do not directly know the essence of God." (R. GARRIGOU-LAGRANGE, *Dieu, son existence et sa nature*, 5th ed., p. 69.) It seems that Scotus must be considered here as a precursor of Leibnitz. (A. KOYRÉ, *Essai*, p. 195.)

209. *Ibid.*, A.T., IX, 92 ff.—St. Augustine (*Conf.*, XII, 10) would more easily have doubted his own existence than God's. But it is a far cry from that to thinking that the idea of God suffices to assure us of the positive possibility of the divine essence, and that it is as clear, if not more so ("the most clear and distinct of all those which are in my mind," *Médit. III*, see above, note 147) as that of the triangle or the square.

210. To Mersenne(?), May 27, 1630(?), A.T., I, 152.

211. *Rép. aux premières Objections*, A.T., IX, 90.—Cf. *Rép. aux deuxièmes Objections*: "Finally when God is said to be *inconceivable*, that means in a full and complete conception, which perfectly includes and embraces all that which is in Him, and not in that mediocre and imperfect conception which is within us, but which nevertheless is sufficient to know that He exists." A.T., IX, 110.

212. *Médit. III*, A.T., IX, 37.

213. Malebranche was perfectly conscious of the difficulty. "If the

219

idea of God is only a modification of our mind it is something finite: therefore it does not need an infinite cause. And that is the first proof from the Méditations to break down." H. GOUHIER, *La Philosophie de Malebranche*, p. 270. Gouhier quotes here the *Réponse à la troisième lettre de M. Arnauld*, pp. 98, 99: "M. Arnauld maintains that the perception of the infinite is fundamentally only a finite modality, and that a finite modality is representative of the infinite: and having assumed that, he affirms that Descartes' demonstration is excellent. But how then, can one prove the existence of God by the perception one has of Him? Is it really clear that an infinite cause is needed to give a finite modality to the soul?"

214. *Principes*, I, 26.—Cf. to Mersenne, January 28, 1641: "I have never dealt with the Infinite, except to submit myself to Him." (A.T., III, 293.)

215. "Pausing long enough over this meditation, one gradually acquires a very clear and, if I may say so, intuitive knowledge of intellectual nature in general, the idea of which, being considered without limitation, is that which represents God to us, and with limitations, that of an angel or of a human soul." To XXX, March 1637, A.T., I, 353.—In his conversation with Burman Descartes is to affirm on the contrary that we can draw almost nothing concerning the nature of pure spirits from the knowledge of our soul. (*Göttingen Ms.*, A.T., V, 157.)

216. He occasionally oscillates back and forth in the same text, as in the celebrated letter to the Marquis of Newcastle, March or April, 1649, A.T., V, 136-139.

217. According to St. Thomas evidence is a property of the thing, in the sense that it has its root in the thing, but it only blossoms out in the mind, which actively makes present to itself the thing *qua* object. It is the radical and potential intelligibility of things which thus becomes actual in the mind. Material things are intelligible in potentiality, they must pass into the mind and become one with it by and in the vital act of intellection in order to hold here, in act—either immediately, in self-evident propositions, or mediately, in demonstrated conclusions—that cogent spiritual light which constitutes evidence.

www.ingramcontent.com/pod-product-compliance
Lightning Source LLC
Chambersburg PA
CBHW020851090426
42736CB00008B/338